Bridal Guide

A Complete Guide On How To Plan Your Wedding

Including...

- 22 Chapters covering everything from customs to the honeymoon
- Summary checklist
- Insuring your valuables
- Gift register
- Invitation list with ideas for wording the invitations
- Sensitive to church/synagogue weddings.
- Comprehensive in discussing the often forgotten extra details for planning a perfect wedding.
- Attractive, easy-to-use format.
- Complete list of music by title, composer, and publisher for easy ordering. Over 400 to choose from.
- A serious, yet creative and thoughtful approach to assisting in the wedding planning.
- Helpful answeres to questions most commonly asked in the 80's.

Plus...

- Helpful hints for the wedding of a second marriage.
- And much, much more...

Bridal Guide

A Complete Guide On How To Plan Your Wedding

Researched and edited
by Pamela Thomas

Bridal Guide, Ltd.,
P.O. Box 2091
La Crosse, Wisconsin 54602
September1989

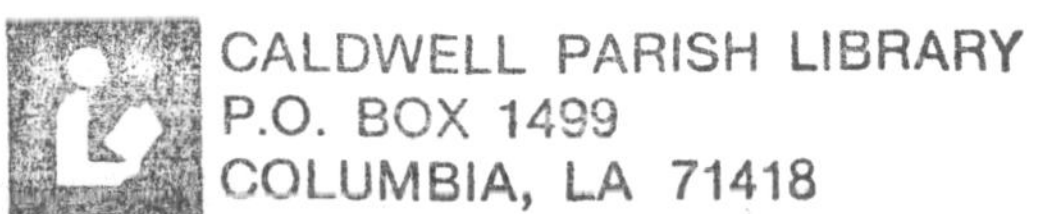

Bridal Guide

First printing	1984	First edition	1984
Second printing	1986	Second edition	1986
Third printing	1987	Third edition	1987
Fourth printing	1989	Fourth edition	1989

Library of Congress: 89-91076
ISBN: 0-9615882-1-7

SAN 697-0729
SAN 697-0737

Printed in the United States of America
by Saint Mary's Press
Terrace Heights, Winona, Minnesota 55987

Dedicated to
my family with love.

Betty and Dale Thomas
Kim Thomas
Nicholas, Brittany, Christopher West

My husband
Richard G. Williams

In memory of
Thelma and Victor Clark
and
Earl "Pete" Thomas

Thank-you.

"Only those who can see the Invisible
can do the Impossible."

TABLE OF CONTENTS

ABOUT THE AUTHOR

A graduate in journalism from Marquette University, Pamela Thomas – Williams has been employed as a copywriter for a variety of advertising agencies, including her own. A winner of several advertising awards, she teamed up with Marian Pellowski in 1983 to devise the best guide to wedding planning. Since that early beginning, Pamela has gone on to meet with many professionals in the bridal industry, and has continued to update each of the editions of Bridal Guide.

Listed in Who's Who of American Women 1988, she is also active in Sigma Delta Chi, PRSA, as well as numerous bridal related associations. Pamela continues her writing and speaking efforts on the topic of weddings with such companies as Bridal Fair, Inc., Globe Communications, Inc., and Carlson-Craft Wedding Invitations.

ACKNOWLEDGEMENTS

The following people contributed greatly to the quality, accuracy of content, marketing, design and support. Thank you.

Sister Luanne Durst
Director
Office of Sacred Worship
Catholic Diocese of La Crosse
La Crosse, Wisconsin

Mrs. Peter Walby
Music Director
Viroqua, Wisconsin

Pastor J.L. Mattes
Clergyman
Good Shepherd English
Evangelical Lutheran Church
La Crosse, Wisconsin

Saul Prombaum (Simcha)
Cantor
Congregations Sons of Abraham
La Crosse, Wisconsin

James Wagner
Executive Director
Catholic Charities, Inc.
Catholic Diocese of La Crosse
La Crosse, Wisconsin

Carlson-Craft Wedding Invitations and Accessories
Mankato, Minnesota

Lyle Boysen
District Sales - Ace Hardware Corp.
Oak Brook, Illinois

Ironwood Press
Typsetting/Printing Consultation
Winona, Minnesota

Brian Desmond
Desmond's Formal Wear
La Crosse, Wisconsin

Charlotte's Bridal
La Crosse, Wisconsin

Anna Hayward
Anna Hayward Designs
Burlington, Ontario, Canada

Gary Kiefner Photography
Photos contributed for use in *Bridal Guide*
La Crosse, Wisconsin

Robert Howard
Cover Design
Santa Barbara, CA

Marian Pellowski
Writing, and research
La Crosse, Wisconsin

Robbi Ernst, III
President June Weddings, Inc.
San Francisco, CA

American Guild of Organists
New York, NY

Kristina Garvin
President/writer
Weatherford Publications
San Francisco, CA

Jack Laak
St. Mary's Press
Winona, Minnesota

INTRODUCTION

Congratulations on your engagement and upcoming marriage! I'm sure you're very excited about the new life you will be starting with the one you love. The next several months will be exciting for you while you make your plans for a perfect wedding day.

There are many details to attend to in coordinating the most cherished day of your life! Written with you, the bride, in mind, our *Bridal Guide* will be a great help in coordinating every aspect of a fabulous wedding day. Please read through it and make notes as you go along. Our book provides ample space to keep track of appointments, expenses, and much more! Carry our *Bridal Guide* with you when shopping for quick reference and to jot things down.

We hope you will enjoy the wealth of information provided herein. Your wedding can be as unique as you want it to be—each person has their own idea of the kind of "day" they want it to be. We can only suggest ways to help you plan every detail. Keep in mind that this book is not intended to cover every aspect of ceremony planning. That must be done with your clergyperson and other professionals involved with the celebration.

Best Wishes and Good Luck for the Future—together!

DISCLAIMER

Bridal Guide, a Complete Guide On How to Plan Your Wedding is designed to be a thorough, step by step handbook for brides and their families to use while planning a wedding. It would be impossible to reprint all the information that is potentially available to the author/publisher, as there are many other resource books that deal with specific needs and types of weddings.

Every effort has been made to make this handbook as complete and as accurate as possible. It is with the assistance of many professionals that have helped to make this book so complete. However, be aware that changes are frequently made and errors are possible.

Hopefully, this book will serve as a guide, and you will find it both informative and interesting to read. The author and publisher shall have neither liability nor responsibility to any person or entity with respect to any loss or damage caused or alleged to be caused directly or indirectly by the information contained here in this book.

Something old,
Something new,
Something borrowed,
Something blue,
And a sixpence in her shoe...

Chapter 1

Origins and Customs

ORIGIN OF THE ENGAGEMENT AND WEDDING RINGS

The ring as a symbol of marriage may have evolved from an African custom where the bride and groom's wrists were tied together with grass during the ceremony. And when grooms negotiated purchase of their brides, they often gave metal rings as partial payment. Eventually, the more precious the metal the wealthier the groom. In ancient Egypt before coins were minted, gold rings were used as currency. To show he trusted his wife with his money, the Egyptian husband placed one of these rings on her finger. The ancients thought that love traveled to the heart in the vein of the third finger of the left hand. To this day, that is still the finger on which the wedding ring is worn. To them, the circle indicated eternity and the iron symbolized lastingness. In any case, the bride received just one ring—upon her engagement. Then, in 1215 the Pope declared a longer waiting period between betrothal and the marriage. So, a second ring, the wedding ring, was placed on the bride's finger during the ceremony when she finally wed.

Another interesting legend is the ring ceremony. During the ceremony the ring was placed on the open Bible. The clergyman then sprinkled it with holy water and blessed it. Then the groom picked it up with his right hand and placed it on the bride's thumb, saying, "In the name of the Father." He then transferred it to the first finger, saying, "And of the Son." Next he changed it to the second finger as he said, "And of the Holy Ghost." Finally he placed it on her finger with "Amen." It did not seem to matter whether the ring was placed on the bride's right or left hand. Sometimes it was placed on the right hand at the espousal and on the left at the wedding ceremony.

ORIGIN OF THE WHITE BRIDAL GOWN

In early Saxon days and through the 18th century, it was the poorer bride who came to her wedding dressed in a plain white robe. This was in the nature of a public statement that she brought nothing with her to her marriage and that therefore her husband was not responsible for her debts. Other brides simply wore their Sunday best. Red was a favorite during the Middle Ages in Europe. Icelandic brides chose black velvet. Colors were chosen for their symbolism as well as for preference. Blue meant constancy; green meant youth. Yellow signified jealousy and therefore was never worn. The brides of ancient Israel wore a blue ribbon on the shoulders of their robes to symbolize purity, fidelity and love. Over the years, the meaning of a white dress symbolized purity. Today, white merely symbolizes the wedding itself—and can be worn by anyone, including the second-time and re-affirming bride.

ORIGIN OF THE BRIDAL VEIL

In Far Eastern countries, people believed that wicked spirits were especially attracted to women. So, as protection from the Evil Eye, women always wore veils. The custom continued although the feeling behind it changed with time into a role of modesty and obedience. From this the veil developed into a symbol of chastity. Then it became the sign of submission of women.

The introduction of the veil into Europe came through returning Crusaders. In early wedding traditions in Europe, the bride was bargained for through her father, was swathed in a bridal veil, and revealed to her mate after the ceremony!

In early centuries, Hebrew, Greek and Roman brides wore veils of many colors, and veils threaded with gold and silver. In Southern Europe, early Christians placed a large cloth over both the bride and groom. In Anglo-Saxon times, the bride wore her hair hanging loose as part of the wedding ritual. The Chinese held a sacred umbrella over the bride's head. Around 1500 in Europe, there was a fashionable conical headdress topped with a veil that hung to the toes. Each era has revealed a different style for the bridal veil.

Nellie Custis was the first American woman to wear a long, white veil of lace when she married Lawrence Lewis, an aide to President Washington. Nellie chose lace because the Major had once glimpsed her face through the lace curtains of an open window—and then afterwards he couldn't stop telling her how beautiful she had looked!

The veil has traditionally stood for youth and virginity.

ORIGIN OF THROWING RICE, OLD SHOES , ETC.

In the days when people lived off the land, their existence depended upon having a good harvest and enough children to help with all the work. Primitive people believed the bride and groom spread good luck on their wedding day. Anyone or anything that touched them would also be lucky. So they showered the couple with ripe grain or nuts, wishing a large harvest for themselves and a large family for the newlyweds. The throwing of grain seemed to symbolize good luck, fertility or abundance. To this day, wedding guests throw rice, grain, confetti, birdseed, etc.

Among the ancient Assyrians and Jews, when a bargain was made, a man gave his sandal as an indication of good faith. A shoe was the symbol of authority. When the Anglo-Saxons hurled a shoe, it indicated that authority had been transferred. Some authorities believe that the throwing of a shoe can be traced back to the missiles which the bride's father hurled at the robber caveman.

ORIGIN OF FLOWERS FOR THE WEDDING PARTY

Throughout history, most celebrations of weddings used flowers in some way. Almost every country has its own traditions and symbolism concerning flowers.

Customs associate the orange blossom most closely with the wedding ceremony. The wearing of a wreath of orange blossoms as a crown over the bridal veil was a Saracen custom introduced by returning Crusaders. Orange blossoms were so expensive that only the wealthy could afford them and poorer brides resorted to artificial ones. A "kissing knot" of croton leaves and rosemary was hung over the bridal couple in Elizabethan England. In Sweden it was believed necessary to put chives, garlic or rosemary in the bride's bouquet to keep the dwarfs from bothering her on her wedding day. In Poland it was believed that to sprinkle the bride's bouquet with sugar would keep her temper sweet. In Rome, roses and marigolds were used to decorate the bride's home. Below are some "meanings" associated with certain flowers:

Apple blossoms or quince blossoms—better things to come
Clematis—love vine
Ivy—good luck
Rosebud—a promise
Myrtle—lover's flower
Laurel—peace
Tulips—infidelity
Yellow flowers of any kind—jealousy
Orange blossoms—fertility

Like the colors of the rainbow...
Our lives will blend in Love

Heather and sweet basil—fortune
Baby's breath—fertility
Cabbage roses—richness of spirit
Anemones—hope
Lily of the Valley—happiness
Red and white roses—unity in love
Lilacs—youthful love
Pansies, forget-me-nots, white clover—special friendship

ORIGIN OF THE WEDDING CAKE

The wedding cake has always been an important part of any wedding feast. Where or when it first originated cannot really be told since it is such an ancient custom. Among certain American Indian tribes, and among the Fiji Islanders, a bride offered her husband a cake of meal. The Romans broke a cake made of salted meal over the bride's head as a symbol of abundance, or fertility. Many people of various nations customarily dropped wheat, flour or cake upon the bride's head, then ate these offerings for good luck. The early Britons baked large baskets of small dry crackers for weddings, and every guest took one home—thus, the tradition of taking wedding cake home to "dream on." During the Middle Ages, it was traditional for the bride and groom to kiss over a pile of small cakes. The small cakes gradually increased in size and richness. Then an enterprising young baker decided to mass all these cakes together and cover them with frosting, thus the modern tiered wedding cake was born.

CULTURAL CUSTOMS

Every culture has its own charming wedding customs. Use your imagination and adapt one from the land of your ancestors. We've researched a few and a librarian will help you probe further.

Africa

"Mayst thou bear 12 children with him" is still the common salutation to brides in remote areas. Many tribes marry the couple by binding their wrists with plaited grass.

Afro-American

On antebellum plantations, brides believed Tuesday and Wednesday weddings guaranteed them a good husband, long lives and happy days.

Bermuda

Newlyweds plant a small tree in their garden. As it grows and strengthens, it symbolizes their love.

Belgium

Brides carry a handkerchief embroidered with their name. After the ceremony, it's framed and displayed until the next family bride adds her name.

China

Two goblets of honey and wine are joined with a red ribbon—the centuries-old color of love and joy—and the couple exchange a drink of unity.

Czechoslovakia

Brides wear wreaths of rosemary for wisdom, love and loyalty.

England

A country bride and her wedding party walk to church on a carpet of blossoms to assure a happy path through life.

Finland

A bride once wore a golden crown during the ceremony. Later she was blindfolded while unmarried women danced around her. Whomever she crowned was predicted to be the next bride.

France

The bride and groom drink a reception toast from an engraved silver two-handled cup, called a "coupe de marriage," and pass it on to future generations.

Germany

On the eve of the wedding, friends of the bride smash pottery at her door. The loud noise is said to avert bad luck. To be sure of future bliss, the bride must sweep it up by herself.

Greece

Couples hold candles decorated with ribbons and flowers.

Holland

A bride and groom sit on thrones under an evergreen canopy—for everlasting love—during a pre-wedding party given by the family. One by one guests approach and offer good wishes.

India

The groom's brother sprinkles flower petals on the couple at conclusion of ceremony. Each family has prepared puffed rice which is mixed during the ceremony for prosperity and fertility.

Iran

In Persian times, the groom bought ten yards of white sheeting to wrap around the bride as a wedding dress.

Ireland

December 31 is considered the luckiest day for weddings in the Ould Sod.

Italy

Since Roman times, couples have walked through the village passing out cakes and sweets.

Japan

The bride and groom take nine sips of sake, becoming husband and wife after the first sip.

Israel

For centuries, couples have had a marriage contract in the form of written vows, called a *ketubbah,* which is embellished by an artisan with bible verses and decorative borders symbolizing the home.

Lithuania

Parents of the couple serve them symbols of married life: wine for joy, salt for tears and bread for work.

Mexico

A white silk cord is draped around the couple's shoulders to indicate their union. Later, guests hold hands in a heart-shaped circle while the newlyweds dance in the center.

Philippines

The white silk cord custom is practiced here as well as in Mexico. All wedding expenses are met by the groom's family, who give the bride old coins symbolizing prosperity. The bride's family presents the newlyweds with a cash dowry.

Poland

Brides wear embroidered white aprons over their gowns. Guests discreetly tuck money into the pockets of the aprons.

Rumania

Wedding guests toss sweets and nuts at the couple to wish them prosperity.

Russia

Wedding guests, other than family, receive gifts rather than give them.

Spain

Brides wear mantillas and orange blossoms in their hair. Grooms wear a tucked shirt hand-embroidered by the bride.

Sweden

Brides carry fragrant herb bouquets to frighten away trolls and grooms have thyme sewn into their wedding suits.

Switzerland

Junior bridesmaids lead the procession tossing colored handkerchiefs to the guests. Whoever catches one contributes money for the couple's nest egg.

U.S.A.

Early Americans gave the honeymooners sack posset, hot spiced milk and brew drink to keep up their energy.

Wales

Brides give attendants cuttings of aromatic myrtle. When one blooms, it foretells another wedding.

TRADITIONS

Trinkets of gold and silver (sometimes quite valuable) are wrapped in waxed paper or foil and often baked in one tier of the bride's cake, or inserted from the bottom after baking. These are intended only for the bridal party—the bridesmaid's gifts are on the left, and groomsmen's are on the right.

Usually the bottom tier of the cake is used, and when the trinkets are placed inside, a marking such as an extra blossom bud, or a piece of white satin ribbon is used to indicate where the surprises are. Traditionally, the following "fortunes' are signified by each trinket:

For the bridesmaids:
- Wishbone—luck
- Heart—romance
- Cat—old maid
- Ring—next to marry
- Dime—fortune
- Thimble or miniature scissors—industry

For the groomsmen:
- A button or dog—bachelor
- A man's wedding ring—next to marry
- Gold coin—money
- Dice—luck

ORIGIN OF TOSSING THE BOUQUET OR GARTER

Originally, it was not a bouquet, but a garter that was tossed. This custom of tossing the garter originated in 14th Century France. For a time a stocking was tossed, but its removal was not easy or graceful. Finally some bride thought of tossing her bouquet and this custom has been followed ever since. Of course, to this day, the gal that catches the bouquet is predicted to be the next to marry, and the guy that catches the garter will be the next guy to get married!

ORIGIN OF THE HONEYMOON

The first marriages were by capture, not choice. When early man felt it was time to take a bride, he carried off an unwilling woman to a secret place where her parents or relatives wouldn't find them. While the moon went through all its phases—about 30 days—they hid from the searchers and drank a brew made from mead and honey. Therefore, we get the word honeymoon. Today, this has come to be a time for the couple to get away to relax and enjoy each other after the hectic schedule of preparing for the wedding.

The
more love
is shared
the more
quickly it
grows

NOTES

Marriage
is
the golden ring
in a chain
whose
beginning
is a glance
and
whose ending
is
Eternity

Kahlil Gibran

Chapter 2

Rings

RINGS

There is no substitute for a reliable, reputable jeweler when selecting your rings. His expertise will help you make your selection to ensure that you will be happy and satisfied for years to come.

It is suggested that you and your fiance decide together on the engagement ring, since you probably have already established preferences as to cut, style, etc. At this time, you may also wish to select your wedding rings.

There are basically three different metals to choose from—gold, platinum, and palladium. Gold is the most used ring metal and is available in a yellow or white color. Pure gold (24K) is too soft for rings. Gold ring settings are usually 14K or 18K alloys of gold and other stronger metals. Platinum is a white metal, which is very expensive. It is the strongest ring metal available and is often used for the prongs which hold the stones in rings of gold. Palladium is similar to platinum in color and strength, but is lighter in weight and costs less.

Of course, the design you choose will depend on your personal preference. A narrow band with a solitaire (single stone) is fitting for a tiny hand, whereas a larger hand can accommodate a cluster of stones. Most jewelers have a wide selection for you to choose from to see what style is best for you, and your budget.

Four basic things to look for when selecting your diamond are color, clarity, cut and carat. The clearer the diamond, the greater its value. Diamonds that are clear and colorless or of a faint blue are considered to be perfect. As the stone's degree of color increases, the value decreases. The degree to which the stone is free from interior or exterior flaws will determine its clarity. The sparkle of a diamond depends on the cut and design used. Diamond cutting is a precise and delicate process during which nearly half of the rough diamond is lost. There are several cuts or designs available—marquise, oval, emerald cut, single cut, baguette, heart-shaped, or pear. Carats deal with the size of the diamond. One carat is equivalent to 100 points.

An engagement ring does not have to be a diamond. You may wish to choose from some of the other semi-precious stones available. For example, you may want your birthstone, or a ruby, emerald, sapphire, opal, or pearl—just to name a few.

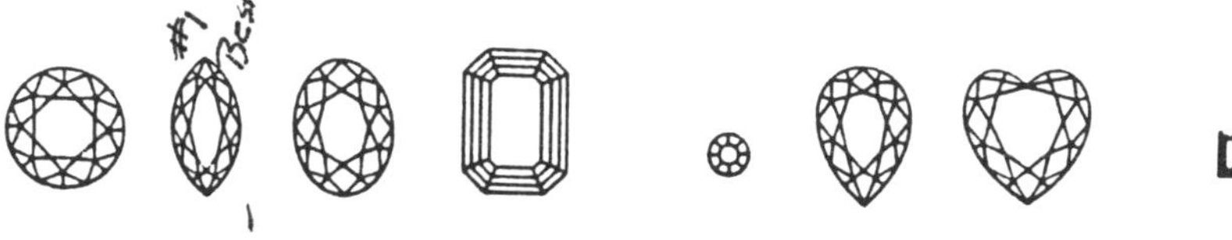

Brilliant • Marquise • Oval • Emerald Cut • Single Cut • Pear • Heart Shape • Baquette

BIRTHSTONES AND THEIR SIGNIFICANCE

January	Garnet or Hyacinth	Constancy
February	Amethyst	Sincerity
March	Bloodstone or Aquamarine	Courage
April	Diamond	Innocence or enduring love
May	Emerald	Success in love
June	Pearl, Moonstone or Agate	Health and long life
July	Ruby or Onyx	Contentment
August	Sardonyx, Peridot, or Carnelian	Felicity
September	Sapphire	Love
October	Opal or Tourmaline	Hope
November	Topaz	Fidelity
December	Turquoise or Lapis Lazuli	Prosperity

In addition to the traditional birthstones assigned to the months of the year, certain stones also are assigned to the days of the week:

Sunday	Topaz or diamond
Monday	Pearl or crystal
Tuesday	Ruby or emerald
Wednesday	Amethyst or loadstone
Thursday	Sapphire or carnelian
Friday	Emerald or cat's-eye
Saturday	Turquoise or diamond

Again, your knowledgeable jeweler will be able to help you make the right decision when selecting your rings so that it will express your personality and be unique for you to enjoy for a lifetime!

Now that you have made the big decision, you will certainly want to take care of this precious treasure. First of all, be sure your ring is insured—either under your parents' insurance policy, or your renter's/homeowner's insurance policy—in case of theft or loss. Below are some tips to keep your jewelry brilliant and sparkling for years to come:

* Remove rings when doing housework; bleaches and cleansers can pit or discolor mountings.
* Diamonds can scratch things, so wrap them separately in tissue paper when traveling. At home, store rings on a ring holder.
* Remove rings during sports activites or heavy work to lessen the chance of losing.
* Have your jeweler check your stone and mounting at least once a year.
* Clean your ring at least once a month:
  —Use liquid detergent and warm water, then brush gently (use small brush). Put rings, earrings, etc., in a wire tea strainer to protect them while rinsing under warm running water. Dry with a soft cloth.
  —Or use equal amounts of cold water and household ammonia. Soak for 30 minutes. Lift out, tap off liquid around the mounting, dip again and drain on paper towel to air-dry.
  —Or you may choose to use a commercial jewelry cleaner.
* Also, keep your hands and nails well manicured because everyone will want to see that beautiful diamond!

NOTES

Love...
is patient and kind; love is not jealous or conceited, or proud or provoked; love does not keep a record of wrongs; love is not happy with evil, but is pleased with the truth. Love never gives up; its faith, hope and patience never fail.

1 Corinthians 13

Chapter 3

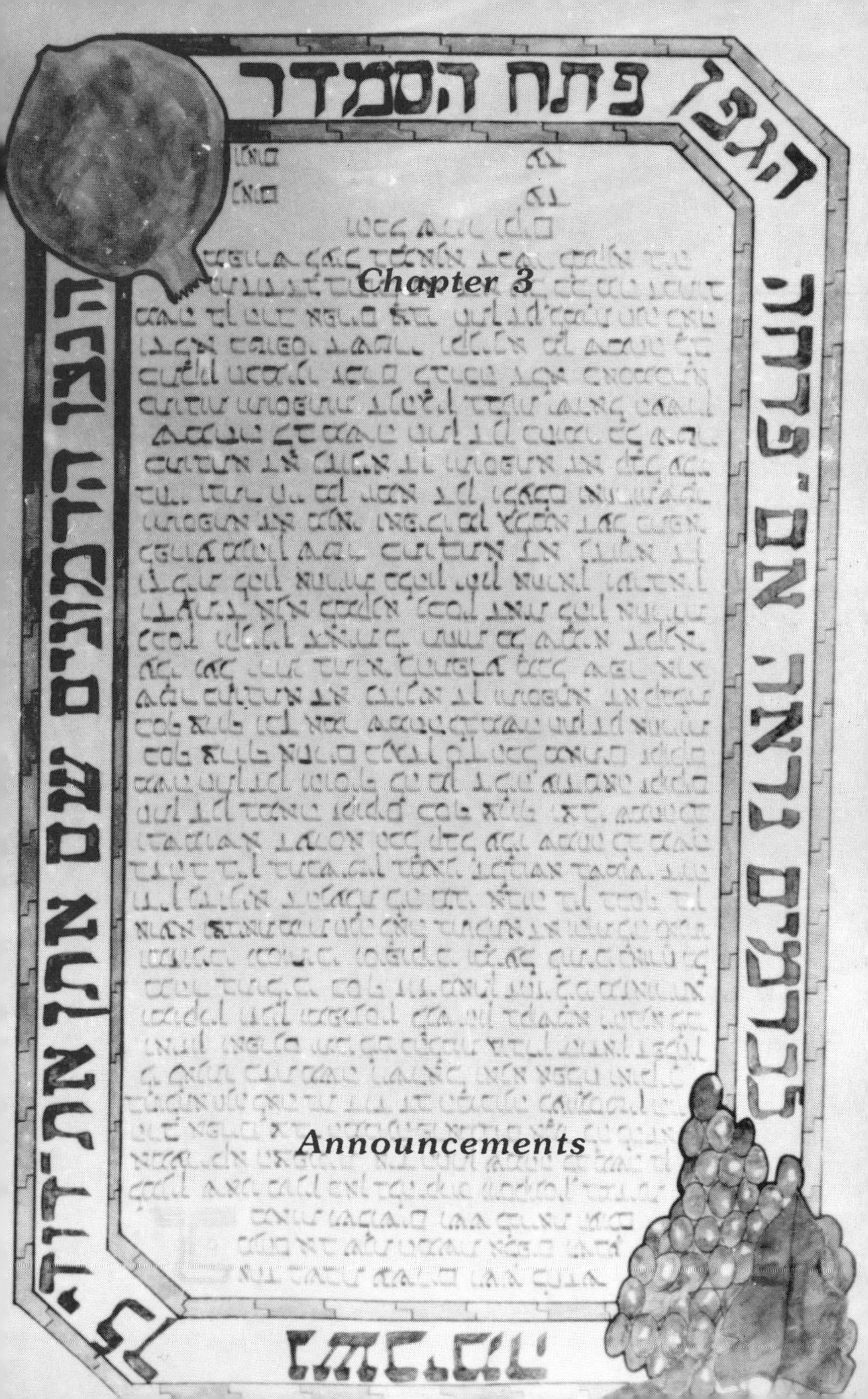

Announcements

WRITING YOUR ANNOUNCEMENT FOR THE NEWSPAPER

An otherwise memorable occasion may be marred if the newspaper account of your engagement/wedding is incorrect. This could involve something as minor as misspelling the name of one of your bridesmaids, or it could be as major as your having married the wrong groom. Because many errors can be traced to confusing information, omissions, or illegible handwriting, it's very important that the person submitting the story or wedding form be very clear on all the details. To avoid confusion and disappointment, here are some tips on how to help the newspaper publish the right information.

Announcements should be sent to your hometown newspaper and your fiance's (if he lives elsewhere). If you have many relatives living in another community, include that paper and do the same for your fiance. Obtain copies of the newspapers in which you plan to insert your announcement in to help you tailor your story to their style. Also obtain information as to what each newspaper requires.

Following are **sample forms** that a newspaper may ask you to fill out:

ENGAGEMENT FORM RULES

1. Each couple may choose to have either an engagement or wedding photo published. If the choice is an engagement photo, it may be submitted within the six months preceding the wedding.
2. Write name on back of photo and clip to this form.
3. Engagement announcements submitted without a photo may be printed at any time up to one month prior to the wedding.
4. Fill out the form using complete legal names (no nicknames).

WEDDING FORM RULES

1. Each couple may choose to have either an engagement or wedding photo published. Photo must be of the couple.
2. Quality black and white photos of the couple are preferred. It is suggested a close-up portrait of the couple (head and shoulder picture) be submitted.
3. Fill out the form using complete legal names (no nicknames).
4. Write name on back of photo and clip to the form.
5. Return the form to the newspaper.

WEDDING FORM

Read the rules before typing or printing information on form.

______________________ ______________________
bride's last name bridegroom's last name

______________________ and ______________________ were
bride's full name bridegroom's full name

married ______________________ , in ______________________
(date and day of week) church (complete name)

__________ , __________ , __________ , by Rev. ______________________ .
city state minister's full name

Parents of the couple are ______________________ , ______________________ ,
her parents address

__________ , ______________________ and ______________________ ,
city state his parents

______________________ , ______________________ , ______________________ ,
address city state

Attending the couple were (full names please, check spellings):

______________________ , ______________________ , ______________________ ,
______________________ , ______________________ , ______________________ ,
______________________ , ______________________ , ______________________ ,

and ______________________ . Guests were seated by ______________________

and ______________________ .

The bride is employed by/attends ______________________
(circle one) name of firm/school

______________________ , __________ , and the bridegroom is employed
city state

by/attends ______________________ , ______________________ ,
(circle one) name of firm/school city

______________________ . Following a wedding trip to ______________________
state

______________________ , the newlyweds will live in ______________________ .
city state

Will a photo be submitted? __________ If so, name of photographer __________

______________________ .

Signature ______________________ Phone No. ______________________

NOTES

Our Love
extends beyond
the reach of time;
beyond the
span of
days and years
it goes
forever

D. Stewart

Chapter 4

Calendars

BRIDE'S CALENDAR

SIX MONTHS TO TWELVE MONTHS BEFORE WEDDING

___ Purchase a wedding planner (or guide) such as this one.
___ Discuss type of wedding you want—formal or informal.
___ Discuss time of day and type of reception.
___ Discuss place of wedding and reception.
___ Discuss wedding budget (include parents).
___ Decide date.
___ Determine number of guests.
___ Visit clergyperson or judge, with fiance.
___ Decide number of wedding party—bridesmaids, groomsmen, personal attendant, etc. Choose them.
___ Plan color scheme for your wedding.
___ Reserve church.
___ Reserve reception hall and caterer.
___ Select and order dresses and accessories.
___ Select and order **your** dress and acessories.
___ Begin guest list for both sides.
___ Register with Bridal Gift Registry at your favorite stores.
___ Plan your new home—where you're going to live and furnishings.
___ Send for honeymoon brochures, or visit your local travel agent.
___ Order rings.
___ Select and reserve photographer and/or videographer.
___ Select florist.
___ Select music for ceremony and reception, or dance. Where appropriate, meet with the liturgy and/or music ministers to plan the music in accord with the liturgical demands of the wedding celebration – very important.
___ Choose ushers.
___ Plan to take the PMI (Pre-Marriage Inventory) or Pre-marriage counseling with the priest, minister, rabbi or trained parish couple.

THREE MONTHS BEFORE WEDDING

___ Complete guest list.

___ Order invitations, thank you cards, napkins, personal stationery, placecards, ceremony programs, wedding album, guest book , etc.
___ Shop for trousseau.
___ Confirm date of delivery on dresses.
___ Confirm date with photographer/videographer.
___ Confirm date with florist.
___ Confirm date with caterer.
___ Confirm date with musician.
___ Confirm church/synagogue arrangements.
___ Make honeymoon reservations.
___ Make appointment with doctor for complete physical. Arrange for blood test if required in your state.
___ Set dates for attending pre-marriage programs set by the local church where required.
___ Make transportation arrangements.
___ Shop for mother's attire.
___ Order wedding attire for men.
___ Arrange attendant's fittings.
___ Start addressing invitations.

TWO MONTHS BEFORE WEDDING

___ Finish addressing invitations. Mail if you have R.S.V.P'S.
___ Plan bridemaid's luncheon.
___ Plan rehearsal dinner.
___ Make arrangements with your fiance to go get marriage license.
___ Plan recording and displaying of gifts received.
___ Order wedding cake.

ONE MONTH BEFORE WEDDING

___ Final fittings with shoes and accessories.
___ Plan bachelor party and bridesmaid's party.
___ Make hotel reservations, or lodging for out-of-town guests.
___ Make appointments for entire wedding party at beauty salon.
___ Mail your invitations.
___ Finalize rehearsal dinner plans.
___ Have formal portrait taken.
___ Finalize transportation arrangements.

___ Send wedding announcement and bridal portrait to your local paper.
___ Look into new insurance coverage, or make necessary policy changes.
___ Change name on driver's license (give effective date).
___ Change name on social security card (give effective date).
___ Change name on charge accounts (credit cards, etc.) — give effective date.
___ Change name on bank accounts (give effective date).
___ Write thank you cards as gifts are received.

Two Weeks Before Wedding

___ Go with fiance for marriage license.
___ Decide on seating arrangement for reception/bridal party.
___ Write out placecards.
___ Notify post office of new address and effective date.
___ Get your new home in order.
___ Have phone installed.
___ Finalize and double-check **all** arrangements.

One Week Before Wedding

___ Confirm rehearsal plans.
___ Pack for honeymoon.
___ Inform attendants of any special responsibilities.

Day Before Wedding

___ RELAX AND ENJOY YOUR SPECIAL DAY!

Groom's Calendar

The groom traditionally has fewer responsibilities than the bride when planning for the wedding, but his involvement is very important. Below is a list of things he will need to do:

Six Months Before Wedding

___ Order bride's engagement/wedding rings.
___ Start making out your guest list.
___ Arrange a visit with clergyperson , or justice of the peace.
___ If you'll share wedding expenses, discuss with fiancee and parents.

___ Discuss with your fiancé how many ushers you will need (about one for every 50 guests) and begin to select them.
___ Discuss honeymoon plans with your fiancee and start making transportation and accommodation reservations.
___ If you are traveling abroad, be sure to update your passport, arrange for visas, and check on innoculations.

THREE MONTHS BEFORE WEDDING

___ Complete your guest list and give it to your fiancee.
___ Discuss and order wedding attire.
___ Decide who you want as your best man and ushers, invite them to participate.
___ Discuss with male attendants their wedding attire.
___ Complete honeymoon plans, buy tickets.

ONE MONTH BEFORE WEDDING

___ Decide on bride's bouquet and going-away corsage; check with fiancee on boutonnieres for men in the wedding party and mothers' corsages.
___ Pick up bride's ring; check engraving.
___ Arrange lodging for relatives and ushers from out-of-town.
___ Select gift for your bride and attendants.
___ Make sure necessary documents—legal, medical, religious—are in order.
___ Make sure all attendants and ushers have ordered their attire.

TWO WEEKS BEFORE WEDDING

___ Make a date with your fiancee to get the marriage license.
___ Check on arrangements for the bachelor dinner (if you are giving it).
___ Arrange with your best man for transportation from the reception to the airport (or from wherever you are planning to leave on your honeymoon).
___ Double-check honeymoon reservations.

ONE WEEK BEFORE WEDDING

___ Present gifts to your attendants (at the bachelor party).
___ Remind your best man and ushers of the rehearsal time and place, and fill them in on rehearsal dinner details.

___ Explain any special seating arrangements to the head usher.
___ Put the clergyperson's or judge's fee in a sealed envelope and give it to the best man. (He will deliver it).
___ Get your going-away clothes ready so you can change after the reception.
___ Pack for your honeymoon.
___ Arrange to move belongings to your new home.

DAY BEFORE WEDDING

___ RELAX AND ENJOY YOUR SPECIAL DAY!

BRIDAL/WEDDING CONSULTANTS

With the busy schedule of families today, many are hiring the sevices of a professional bridal consultant. This person assumes all of the responsibilities of the wedding – from attire and planning to the reception and transportation. He or she will be the authority on all of the aspects of the wedding planning and will be able to carry out all of the details from beginning to end

Remember, however, that this is your wedding day. You and your family should have everything you want. A good wedding consultant knows that.

For more information, contact: Robbi Ernst III at June Weddings, Inc. Phone (415) 989–0120.

NOTES

___

___

___

___

___

___

___

___

___

Love is
the most
beautiful gift
we are given
to share

Chapter 5

Paying for the Expenses

WHO PAYS FOR WHAT

There aren't any absolute rules as to who pays for what. Traditionally, wedding expenses have been taken care of by the bride's family, with the groom responsible for the rings and the honeymoon. While tradition is still an honored part of our heritage, financial obligations must often give way to everyday realities and compromise. At the time of the wedding planning, both sets of parents, along with the engaged couple, should meet to discuss the financial arrangements. It is wise for each party to make any financial limits absolutely clear—to prevent misunderstandings or hard feelings at a later date after definite plans have been made. If the parents of the groom are financially willing and able, they may offer at any time to pay part, half, or all of the wedding expenses.

Below is a traditional list of who pays for what, but the final decision really depends on who is most willing and able to pay.

THE BRIDE

___ Wedding ring for the groom (if it's a double ring ceremony).
___ A wedding gift for the groom.
___ Presents for the bridal attendants.
___ Personal stationery.
___ Accommodations for her out-of-town attendants.
___ Physical examination and blood test.

THE GROOM

___ The bride's rings.
___ Wedding gift for the bride.
___ The marriage license.
___ Gifts for best man and ushers.
___ Flowers—bride's bouquet and going-away corsage; corsages for mothers; boutonnieres for men in wedding party.
___ Accommodations for out-of-town ushers or best man.
___ His blood test.
___ Gloves, ties, or ascots for the men in the wedding party.
___ Fee for the clergyperson/judge.
___ The honeymoon.
___ Bachelor dinner (optional).

The Bride's Family

___ The entire cost of the reception: rental of hall, if reception is not held at home; caterer; food (including wedding cake); beverages; gratuities for bartenders, waiters; decorations; music; flowers.
___ A wedding gift for the newlyweds.
___ The bride's wedding attire/trousseau.
___ The wedding invitations, announcements, thank you's, napkins, etc., and mailing costs.
___ The fee for engagement and wedding photographs.
___ Ceremony—rental of sanctuary; fees for organist, soloist, or choir, etc.; aisle carpets; and any other costs for decorations.
___ Bridesmaids' bouquets.
___ Gratuities for policeman directing traffic and /or parking.
___ Transportation for bridal party from the bride's house to the wedding ceremony, and from the ceremony to the reception.
___ Bridesmaids' luncheon.
___ Rehearsal dinner (optional).
___ Household furnishings for bride and groom—from linens, china, silver, and crystal to furniture (optional).

The Groom's Family

___ Clothes for the wedding.
___ Any traveling expenses and hotel bills they incur.
___ Wedding gift for the newlyweds.
___ Rehearsal dinner, or any other expenses they elect to assume (optional).

The Attendants

___ Their wedding clothes.
___ Any traveling expenses they incur.
___ Wedding gift for the newlyweds.

The Guests

___ Any traveling expenses and hotel bills they incur.
___ Wedding gift for the newlyweds.

NOTES

Love gives us the freedom
to share ourselves completely
in the deepest kind
of friendship

Chapter 6

Budgeting

THE BUDGET

The Ceremony	Estimated Cost	Actual Cost
Church or ceremony site	$____	$____
Officiator	$____	$____
Organist	$____	$____
Musicians	$____	$____
Soloist	$____	$____
Aisle runner	$____	$____
Candles, Wedding candle	$____	$____
Canopy	$____	$____
Decorations (other than flowers)	$____	$____
Other expenses...	$____	$____
PMI (Pre-Marriage Inventory)	$____	$____
____________	$____	$____
____________	$____	$____
____________	$____	$____
TOTALS	$____	$____

The Reception	Estimated Cost	Actual Cost
Hall rental	$____	$____
Cake	$____	$____
Food	$____	$____
Entertainment	$____	$____
Liquor	$____	$____
Decorations (other than flowers)	$____	$____
Other expenses...	$____	$____
____________	$____	$____
____________	$____	$____
____________	$____	$____
TOTALS	$____	$____

The Photographer/Videographer

	Estimated Cost	Actual Cost
Formal engagement	$	$
Glossy (engagement)	$	$
Formal wedding	$	$
Glossy (wedding)	$	$
Album	$	$
Candids	$	$
Edited tape	$	$
Unedited tape	$	$
Other expenses...		
______	$	$
______	$	$
______	$	$
______	$	$
TOTALS	$	$

The Stationery

	Estimated Cost	Actual Cost
Invitations/Announcements	$	$
R.S.V.P'S	$	$
Thank – You's	$	$
Printed napkins	$	$
Matches	$	$
Cake boxes	$	$
Guest book	$	$
Ceremony programs	$	$
Reception favors	$	$
Possibly decorations	$	$
Other expenses...		
______	$	$
______	$	$
______	$	$
TOTALS	$	$

The Flowers	Estimated Cost	Actual Cost
(CEREMONY SITE)		
Altar	$	$
(except in Catholic churches)		
Pew markers	$	$
Bride's bouquet	$	$
Attendants' bouquets	$	$
Boutonnieres	$	$
Corsages	$	$
Possibly the aisle runner	$	$
(RECEPTION SITE)		
Hall	$	$
Buffet table	$	$
Guest tables	$	$
Cake table	$	$
Other expenses...		
	$	$
	$	$
	$	$
	$	$
TOTALS	$	$

The Wedding Attire	Estimated Cost	Actual Cost
Bride's dress	$	$
Headpiece	$	$
Veil	$	$
Shoes	$	$
Lingerie	$	$
Jewelry	$	$
Accessories	$	$
Other expenses...		
	$	$
	$	$
TOTALS	$	$

The Gifts	Estimated Cost	Actual Cost
Groom	$______	$______
Groom's ring bearer	$______	$______
Attendants/Ushers	$______	$______
Hostess	$______	$______
Host	$______	$______
Guest book attendant	$______	$______
Cake server	$______	$______
Personal attendant	$______	$______
Other expenses		
________________	$______	$______
________________	$______	$______
________________	$______	$______
________________	$______	$______
TOTALS	$______	$______

The Transportation	Estimated Cost	Actual Cost
Limousine	$______	$______
Parking/Valet	$______	$______
Other expenses...		
________________	$______	$______
________________	$______	$______
TOTALS	$______	$______

Miscellaneous Expenses	Estimated Cost	Actual Cost
________________	$______	$______
________________	$______	$______
________________	$______	$______
________________	$______	$______

______________________	$________	$________
______________________	$________	$________
______________________	$________	$________
______________________	$________	$________
______________________	$________	$________
TOTALS	$________	$________
TOTAL WEDDING COSTS	$________	$________

NOTES

In Spring a young girl's fancy
Is filled with a number of things—
Hearts and flowers and bridal showers
Romance and wedding rings.

Chapter 7

Showers

SHOWERS

The custom of a "bridal shower" came about when a poor Dutch miller fell in love with a maiden whose father forbade the match and refused to provide a dowry. The miller's friends came to the rescue and "showered" the bride-to-be with enough gifts in order to start housekeeping.

The wedding shower, traditionally a get-together for women only, is now just as likely to include the female and male. A "his and her" shower is a perfect way for the bride's friends and the groom's friends to meet each other. It also is easier to plan showers around what both the bride and groom enjoy.

Any friend of the bride and groom may give a shower. Traditionally, it should not be a member of their immediate families. Plan with your friends when selecting a date, as you may be busy during this time with making other plans for your wedding day. Consult with them as to where you are registered for wedding gift ideas. Then you may wish to choose a theme for the shower. Shower theme ideas are given below:

Kitchen Shower — Kitchen showers offer a wide range of gift ideas and prices.

Gadgets/strainers, peelers, etc.
Nonstick-coated cookware/bakeware
Small appliances/clock, electric skillet, coffee maker, electric can opener, hand mixer, crock pot, popcorn maker, deep fryer, etc.
Canister set
Spice rack/spices
Cutlery
Cutting board
Utensil set
Measuring cups/spoons
Mugs
Cookbooks
Salt & pepper shakers
Funnels
Kitchen towels/dish cloths/pot holders/scrub pads/dish soap/laundry soap, etc.
Aprons
Serving bowls, freezer containers, etc.

Bar Shower — Everything the couple will need for stocking a basic home bar.

Assorted liquor
Assorted wines
Assorted liqueurs
Assorted aperitifs
Mixers
Glasses/goblets/snifters
Ice bucket
Cocktail shaker
Wine rack
Bar utensils
A guide to mixing drinks
Carafe
Punch bowl
Pitchers
Coasters
Corkscrew
Blender
Ice crusher

Personal Shower — To pamper the bride and groom at this special time.

Hers

Peignoir sets
Nightgown
Robe
Teddy
Bra & bikini set
Camisole
Slips
Slippers
Padded hangers
Scents/soaps
Sachets
Cologne
Dusting powder
Monogrammed stationery

His

Pajamas
Robe
Terry wrap
Slippers
Razor
Travel alarm
After shave/cologne
Travel kit
Calculator
Stationery

Plant Shower/Gardening Shower

Variety of plants
Pots
Potting soil
Plant fertilizer
Planting utensils
Plant hangers
Gardening tools/gloves/ equipment
Bulbs/seeds
Plant stand
Book about plants

Linen Shower

Tablecloths/table runners
Napkins/napkin rings
Placemats
Dish towels/cloths
Potholder/mitts
Towels/bath, hand, guest
Bath sheets
Washcloths
Accessories
Bath mats
Scale
Sheets
Pillows
Pillowcases
Blankets
Electric blanket
Comforter
Bedspread
Pillow shams
Hamper
Rug and lid set
Shower curtain & liner

Gourmet Shower — A joint shower idea for the couple that enjoys cooking and entertaining.

Wok
Souffle dish
Warming trays
Food processor
Stand mixer
Toaster-oven
Matching aprons
Espresso maker
Hibachi
Molds
Coffee grinder
Poachers
Crepe maker
Vegetable steamer
Assorted prepackaged foods
Vinegars
Preserves
Herbs & spices
Cheese boards/servers
Baskets
Salad spinner
Food slicer
Microwave oven/convection oven
Yogurt maker
Ice cream maker
Juicer
Serving bowls
Recipe books

Joint Gift Ideas

A place setting of fine china
A place setting of sterling
Informal dinnerware
Flatware
Sterling candlesticks
Crystal decanter set
Luggage
Radio
Television
Electronic games
Stereo equipment
Camera/lens
Gas Grill
Sports equipment
Gift certificates
Vacuum cleaner
Garden equipment
Home video equipment

Barbeque Shower

Grill
Barbeque utensils
Charcoal
Lighter fluid
Barbeque guide/recipes

Recipe Shower — Each guest brings a favorite recipe and either some of the ingredients or some of the utensils necessary to make the recipe.

Recipe cards (blank)
Recipe box
Recipe books
Recipe holders

Pantry Shower

Canned goods
Prepared foods
Anything for the kitchen cupboard—staples

Paper Shower

Table mats
Napkins
Paper towels
Magazine subscriptions
Personalized stationery
Book matches

Tupperware Shower

Anything made of Tupperware—containers, etc.

Crystal Shower

Any needed glassware, etc.

Of course, these are just some themes for showers. The list can go on and on, depending on what the couple may need or like. Just let your imagination go to work!

If the couple is beginning marriage with virtually nothing, a general shower is probably the best to give, even if you are including the groom. If they are merging households and need to fill in items, a theme shower is the most practical. This way you can indulge the couple with necessities and luxuries at the same time. In any case, consult the bridal registries, family, and mutual friends for gift suggestions. When you decide the type of shower you will hold, be sure to specify it on the invitations.

The main event at all showers is the bride and groom opening the gifts. Make sure you have one of the hosts or a guest record the gifts and the giver so the bride will have an accurate account when writing out thank you notes. Have someone take snapshots at the shower. This may also be a nice gift from the "photographer." He/she may wish to put together a photo album of the shower.

Refreshments served will depend on the time of day you plan to hold the shower. Keep refreshments as simple as possible. Salads, casseroles, cold cuts, barbeques, sandwiches, etc., are the easiest to make and can be done ahead of time.

NOTES

How beautiful
life can be
When touched
by love

Chapter 8

Bridal Gift Registry

THE BRIDAL GIFT REGISTRY

The bridal gift registry is a free service offered by department and specialty stores that gives you the opportunity to list the items you really need and want. It makes it easier for your guests to select a gift because they know that their choice is something you really want. You will also avoid getting gifts that are not compatible with your life-style and also avoid getting duplicates that will have to be exchanged. You should register at your favorite shops soon after you become engaged. This will be helpful to guests that will be invited to your engagement parties or showers. Many people are offended by giving money gifts. It is important to register!

Do some homework ahead of time when choosing your items for your new home. Choose these things together with your fiance, since both of you will be sharing them. Look through magazines, newspapers, stores, etc., to decide what patterns and styles you like. Then visit your bridal gift registrar who will be able to help you with any questions you may have about coordinating all the elements that go into furnishing and accessorizing your new home.

Following is a helpful guide to use when selecting your items. Also, be sure to let your registry places know when you receive an item, so they can take it off your list to avoid duplicates. Be aware that some stores offer a **Bride** and a **Groom** Registry.

LINENS

Before you register your pattern and requirements of your furniture for bedroom and dining room linen it is wise to know dimensions. Is your bed double, queen, or king-size? Is your dining room table rectangular, square, or round? What does it measure at its smallest dimension, and what does it measure when all the leaves are added?

My bed linen pattern is ________________ .
My bed size is ____________ .
My pillow size is ____________ .
My dining room table measures ______ (closed), and ______ (open).
My kitchen table measures ________ (closed), and ________ (open).

This day
I will marry my friend:
The one I laugh with, live for,
dream with, Love

TABLE & OTHER KITCHEN LINEN

	Size	Color	Quantity Required	Quantity Received
Tablecloths				
Runners				
Napkins				
Napkin rings				
Placemats				
Dish towels				
Dishcloths				
Pot holders/mitts				
Aprons				
Appliance covers				

BATHROOM LINENS

	Size	Color	Quantity Required	Quantity Received
Bath sheets				
Bath towels				
Hand towels				
Washcloths				
Guest towels				
Bath mat				
Rug/lid set				
Shower curtain				
Scale				
Hamper				
Other				

BEDROOM LINENS

	Size	Color	Quantity Required	Quantity Received
Flat sheets				
Fitted sheets				
Pillowcases/shams				
Pillows				
Blankets				
Bedspread				
Comforter/quilt				
Mattress pads/ protectors				
Pillow protectors				
Electric blanket				

Dinnerware

My FORMAL Dinner is ____________________

By ____________________

Service for ____________________

My CASUAL Dinner ware is ____________________

By ____________________

Service for ____________________

Quantity Required	Quantity Received		Quantity Received	Quantity Required
____	____	Dinner plates	____	____
____	____	Lunch/salad plates	____	____
____	____	Dessert plates	____	____
____	____	Bread & butter plates	____	____
____	____	Soup bowls	____	____
____	____	Cereal/fruit bowls	____	____
____	____	Tea cup & saucer	____	____
____	____	Coffee Cup & saucer	____	____
____	____	Demitasse & saucer	____	____
____	____	Coffee mug	____	____
____	____	Covered vegetable dish	____	____
____				
____	____	Platter(s)	____	____
____	____	Salad or serving bowl	____	____
____	____	Coffee pot	____	____
____	____	Tea pot	____	____
____	____	Sugar & creamer	____	____
____	____	Gravy boat	____	____
____	____	Salt & pepper shakers	____	____
____	____	Casserole dishes	____	____

NOTES

Serving Accessories

My FORMAL Accessories are ______________________ My CASUAL Accessories are ______________________

By ______________________ By ______________________

Quantity Required	Quantity Received		Quantity Received	Quantity Required
____	____	Chafing dish	____	____
____	____	Compote	____	____
____	____	Coffee service	____	____
____	____	Tea service	____	____
____	____	Serving trays	____	____
____	____	Carafé	____	____
____	____	Pitchers	____	____
____	____	Serving cart	____	____
____	____	Trivets	____	____
____	____	Cake plates	____	____
____	____	Baskets	____	____
____	____	Salad bowls	____	____
____	____	Cheese board	____	____
____	____	Soup tureen	____	____
____	____	Candy dish	____	____
____	____	Platter	____	____
____	____	Candlesticks	____	____

Cooking Equipment & Other Kitchenware

Quantity Required	Quantity Received	
____	____	Saucepans (variety of sizes)
____	____	Skillets (variety of sizes)
____	____	Covered casseroles (variety of sizes)
____	____	Baking dishes (variety of sizes)
____	____	Double boiler
____	____	Stockpot
____	____	Roaster & rack
____	____	Wok
____	____	Dutch oven
____	____	Souffle dishes
____	____	Omelet pan
____	____	Quiche dish
____	____	Cookie sheets
____	____	Muffin tins
____	____	Bread pans

______	______	Cake pans
______	______	Pie plates
______	______	Bundt pan
______	______	Angel food pan
______	______	Fondue pot
______	______	Tea kettle
______	______	Canister set
______	______	Cutlery
______	______	Cutting boards
______	______	Cookie jar
______	______	Utensil set
______	______	Timer
______	______	Food scale
______	______	Mixing bowl
______	______	Storage containers
______	______	Kitchen clock
______	______	Spice rack
______	______	Egg beater
______	______	Can/bottle opener
______	______	Measuring cups
______	______	Measuring spoons
______	______	Grater
______	______	Strainers
______	______	Colander
______	______	Ice cream spoons
______	______	Molds
______	______	Vegetable peeler
______	______	Baster
______	______	Whisks
______	______	Thermometer
______	______	Cheese cutter
______	______	Cookbooks

Stemware

My CRYSTAL Stemware is ______________________

By ______________________

Service for ______________________

My EVERYDAY Stemware is ______________________

By ______________________

Service for ______________________

Quantity Required	Quantity Received		Quantity Received	Quantity Required
____	____	Water goblet	____	____
____	____	Tumbler	____	____
____	____	Fruit juice	____	____
____	____	Iced tea	____	____
____	____	Sherbet	____	____
____	____	Highball	____	____
____	____	Cocktail	____	____
____	____	Old-fashioned	____	____
____	____	Champagne	____	____
____	____	Wine	____	____
____	____	Brandy	____	____
____	____	Beer	____	____
____	____	Pitchers	____	____
____	____	Cordials	____	____
____	____	Decanters	____	____

NOTES

Flatware

My FORMAL Flatware is ________________________

By ________________________

Service for ________________________

My CASUAL Flatware is ________________________

By ________________________

Service for ________________________

Quantity Required (Formal)	Quantity Received (Formal)		Quantity Received (Casual)	Quantity Required (Casual)
______	______	Dinner knives	______	______
______	______	Dinner forks	______	______
______	______	Salad forks	______	______
______	______	Teaspoons	______	______
______	______	Soup spoons	______	______
______	______	Iced tea spoons	______	______
______	______	Serving spoons	______	______
______	______	Gravy ladle	______	______
______	______	Pie/cake server	______	______
______	______	Cake knife	______	______
______	______	Serving fork	______	______
______	______	Pickle fork	______	______
______	______	Cheese serving knife	______	______
______	______	Butter server	______	______
______	______	Butter spreader	______	______
______	______	Silver chest	______	______
______	______	Steaks knives	______	______
______	______	Cutlery set	______	______
______	______	Salad serving set	______	______

NOTES

____

____

____

____

____

____

____

____

____

Small Electric Appliance

Quantity Required	Received	
______	______	Toaster
______	______	Mixer
______	______	Blender
______	______	Food processor
______	______	Coffee maker
______	______	Fry pan/skillet
______	______	Waffle iron/griddle
______	______	Can opener
______	______	Electric knife/food slicer
______	______	Toaster oven
______	______	Warming tray
______	______	Slow cooker/crock pot
______	______	Corn popper
______	______	Ice cream maker
______	______	Pasta maker
______	______	Juicer
______	______	Steamer
______	______	Egg cooker
______	______	Wok
______	______	Microwave/convection oven

NOTES

Miscellaneous Items

Quantity Required	Quantity Received	
______	______	Vacuum cleaner
______	______	Electric broom
______	______	Iron
______	______	Ironing board
______	______	Tool box/tools
______	______	Fire exstinguisher
______	______	Smoke alarm
______	______	Lawn equipment
______	______	Luggage
______	______	Sewing machine
______	______	Barbeque equipment
______	______	Sports equipment
______	______	Furniture
______	______	Area rugs
______	______	Lamps
______	______	Card table/chairs
______	______	TV trays
______	______	Decorative clocks
______	______	Ash trays
______	______	Candles/candle holders
______	______	Vases
______	______	Wall decorations
______	______	Other

NOTES

The path that leads to happiness
is so narrow that two cannot walk on it...
unless they become one

Chapter 9

Marriage License

THE MARRIAGE LICENSE

Marriage license requirements are state-regulated and may be obtained from the Clerk of Courts in most county courthouses. Requirements vary from state to state, but generally include the following:

_______ Applying for and paying the fee for the marriage license. Make your application early enough to allow for any required waiting period before issuance. There is also a waiting period between the time the license is issued and when the ceremony may be performed, and the license must be signed by the officiating person and witnesses. Also determine if the marriage license has an expiration date by which the marriage must be performed.

_______ Meeting of residency requirements of the state and/or county where the ceremony will take place.

_______ Meeting the legal age requirements for both bride and groom, or having parental permission if underage.

_______ Presenting upon application for the license any required identification, birth or baptismal certificates, marriage eligibility or other documents.

_______ Obtaining a medical examination and/or blood test for both bride and groom, used for detection of communicable diseases, particularly venereal. Whether or not this is required, the couple owes it to themselves to begin their married life in good health. This is also an excellent time to discuss any questions on birth control or child-bearing with the doctor.

_______ If you have been married before, you may need to bring a copy of your Divorce Decree.

NOTES

____

____

____

Now we will feel no rain,
for each of us will be
shelter for the other.
Now we will feel no cold,
for each of us will be
warmth to the other.
Now we are two persons,
but there is only
one life before us.
Let us go now to enter into
the days of our life together.

Apache Wedding Blessing

Chapter 10

Invitations

WEDDING INVITATIONS AND ANNOUNCEMENTS

Traditional or contemporary, today's invitations offer a wide variety of options to help set the tone of your wedding. As soon as you and your fiance set a date and guest lists are complete, select and order your invitations. Allow at least three months before your wedding so you will have plenty of time for addressing, mailing, and responses.

Invitations can be ordered from jewelers, stationery stores, department stores, specialty shops, or advertisements in magazines. All have consultants and/or samples to help you in your selection of paper stock, color, design, and lettering style. Invitations can be engraved or thermographed. Thermography is a process that resembles engraving, but is less expensive and more readily available.

When you place your order, ask about getting the outer and inner envelopes ahead of time so that you can have them addressed and ready to mail when the invitations arrive. There may be a small extra charge for this. Wedding invitations are to be mailed four to six weeks prior to the wedding date. They should all be mailed at the same time. Check with your local post office for the amount of postage needed to mail your wedding invitation as postage may vary, depending on number of enclosures.

Envelopes should be handwritten in black ink—never typed. Do not abbreviate names or addresses. Either have the return address printed or do it yourself when you are addressing the envelopes. If you are including a response card be sure it is stamped and pre-addressed.

The inner envelope is left unsealed and addressed to "Mr. and Mrs. Jones," without first names or addresses. Children under sixteen may be included by writing their first names in a line below their parents' on the inner envelope. Older children in the family should receive their own invitation.

If your invitations contain several enclosures, the proper order of placement is as follows: The ungummed envelope contains the invitation along with the other enclosures and is placed in the outer envelope so it faces the flap. Tissue paper is placed over the engraving or printing to ensure against smudging. Response cards are tucked inside the invitation and, if needed, include a map. Be sure it is a clear reproduction on good quality paper. This also belongs inside the invitation with the other enclosures.

Invitations are usually issued by the parents of the bride, or by the surviving parent, or, if the bride is an orphan, by the nearest of kin. The accepted order of kinship is as follows: Elder brother; Elder sister; Both grandparents, or one surviving; Uncle and/or Aunt; Guardian; Bride and groom issue invitations themselves; Groom's family.

The most simple, and inexpensive, system for creating a guest list is a notebook or recipe file divided alphabetically. Begin to fill it in as you plan, gathering addresses as you go. Perhaps even color-coding if they are bride or groom's relatives or friends. The list is equally divided between bride and groom. You can be sure that about 30% will not attend, 50% or more if out-of-town guests. The bottom line on who to invite depends on your budget.

WORDING ETIQUETTE FOR INVITATIONS

* Note: It is preferred that parents of both children be named.

IF INVITATIONS ARE ISSUED BY BRIDE'S PARENTS:
STANDARD FORM

Mr. and Mrs. John William Jones
request the honour of your presence
at the marriage of their daughter
Lynn Marie
to
Mr. Ronald John Adams
on Saturday, the second of June
Nineteen hundred and eighty-four
at two o'clock in the afternoon
American Lutheran Church
Medford, Wisconsin

WEDDING MASS/WEDDING SERVICE

Mr. and Mrs. John William Jones
request the honour of your presence
at the marriage of their daughter
Lynn Marie
to

Mr. Ronald John Adams
on Saturday, the second of June
Nineteen hundred and eighty-four
at an eleven o'clock Wedding Mass
Saint John's Catholic Church
Medford, Wisconsin

WEDDING MASS/WEDDING SERVICE

Mr. and Mrs. John William Jones
request the honour of your presence
at the Wedding Mass (Service)
at which their daughter
Lynn Marie
and
Mr. Ronald John Adams
will be united in the
Sacrament of Marriage
on Saturday, the second of June
Nineteen hundred and eighty-four
at ten o'clock
Saint John's Catholic Church
Medford, Wisconsin

IF MOTHER OR FATHER ARE DECEASED—Living parent not remarried:

Mrs. John William Jones
requests the honour of your presence
at the marriage of her daughter
Lynn Marie

IF LIVING PARENT HAS REMARRIED:

Mr. and Mrs. John R. Jacobs
request the honour of your presence
at the marriage of Mrs. Jacobs' daughter
Lynn Marie

OR

Mr. and Mrs. John R. Jacobs
request the honour of your presence
at the marriage of her daughter
Lynn Marie

OR

Mr. and Mrs. John R. Jacobs
request the honour of your presence
at the marriage of their daughter
Lynn Marie

IF MOTHER AND FATHER ARE DECEASED—Invitations issured by unmarried older brother or sister:

Mr. Roger John Jones
requests the honour of your presence
at the marriage of his sister
Lynn Marie

IF INVITATIONS ARE ISSUED BY MARRIED OLDER BROTHER OR SISTER:

Mr. and Mrs. William P. Evans
request the honour of your presence
at the marriage of her sister
Lynn Marie Jones

IF INVITATIONS ARE ISSUED BY GRANDMOTHER OR UNCLE AND AUNT:

Mr. and Mrs. Warren J. Smith
request the honour of your presence
at the marriage of their granddaughter
Lynn Marie Jones

IF BRIDE AND GROOM ISSUE THEIR OWN INVITATIONS:

The honour of your presence is requested
at the marriage of
Miss Lynn Marie Jones
and
Mr. Ronald John Adams

OR

Miss Lynn Marie Jones
and
Mr. Ronald John Adams
request the honour of your presence
at their marriage

IF INVITATIONS ARE ISSUED BY A FRIEND:

Mr. and Mrs. Steven James Carlson
request the honour of your presence
at the marriage of
Miss Lynn Marie Jones
and
Mr. Ronald John Adams

MOTHER DIVORCED—If not remarried she may use a combination of her maiden name and married name. (This is regarded as an individual decision.)

Mrs. Johnson Jones
requests the honour of your presence
at the marriage of her daughter
Lynn Marie

MOTHER REMARRIED:

Mrs. Thomas C. Renaldo
requests the honour of your presence
at the marriage of her daughter
Lynn Marie Jones

OR

Mr. and Mrs. Thomas C. Renaldo
request the honour of your presence
at the marriage of her daughter
Lynn Marie Jones

OR

Mr. and Mrs. Thomas C. Renaldo
request the honour of your presence
at the marriage of Mrs. Renaldo's daughter
Lynn Marie Jones

IF GROOM'S PARENTS ISSUE INVITATIONS:

Mr. and Mrs. Roger Albert Adams
request the honour of your presence
at the marriage of
Miss Lynn Marie Jones
to their son
Mr. Ronald John Adams

SECOND MARRIAGES—Young divorcee uses combination of maiden and married names:

Mr. and Mrs. John William Jones
request the honour of your presence
at the marriage of their daughter
Lynn Jones Adams

YOUNG WIDOW USES MARRIED NAME:

Mr. and Mrs. John William Jones
request the honour of your presence
at the marriage of their daughter
Lynn Marie Adams

DOUBLE WEDDINGS—When brides are sisters the older sister is mentioned first:

Mr. and Mrs. John William Jones
request the honour of your presence
at the marriage of their daughters
Lynn Marie
to
Mr. Ronald John Adams
and
Mary Lou
to
Mr. Richard David Smith

WHEN THE BRIDES ARE NOT SISTERS THE OLDER BRIDE AND HER FAMILY ARE MENTIONED FIRST:

Mr. and Mrs. John William Jones
and
Mr. and Mrs. Albert Richard Davidson
request the honour of your presence
at the marriage of their daughters
Lynn Marie Jones
to
Mr. Ronald John Adams
and
Sally Ann Davidson
to
Mr. Mark Lee Paulson

RECEPTION INVITATIONS—The phrase "request the pleasure of your company" is used here and on invitations to other social functions.

Mr. and Mrs. John William Jones
request the pleasure of your company
at the wedding reception for their daughter
Lynn Marie
and

Mr. Ronald John Adams
on Saturday, the second of June
Nineteen hundred and eighty-four
at eight o'clock in the evening
1151 Oakwood Drive
Medford, Wisconsin

WEDDING ANNOUNCEMENTS—Announcements must always have a year line, and time of ceremony is never mentioned.

Mr. and Mrs. John William Jones
have the honour of announcing
the marriage of their daughter
Lynn Marie
to
Mr. Ronald John Adams
on Saturday, the second of June
Nineteen hundred and eighty-four
American Lutheran Church
Medford, Wisconsin

OR

Mr. and Mrs. John William Jones
have the honour to announce
the marriage of their daughter

ANNOUNCEMENT FOR MATURE WIDOW:

Mrs. Jane Jones
and
Mr. John T. Smith
have the pleasure of announcing their marriage

TITLES—Reverend, Doctor, Captain, etc. are not abbreviated unless lack of space necessitates it.

SUFFIXES—Jr., junior, II, III, IV, are all properly preceded by a comma. Jr. is capitalized when abbreviated, junior is not capitalized when spelled in full. Roman numerals are properly preceded by a comma.

MILITARY WEDDINGS—Officers above the rank of lieutenant have title preceding name:

Major and Mrs. John William Jones
request the honour of your presence
at the marriage of their daughter
Lynn Marie
to
Captain Ronald John Adams
United States Army

Junior officers have title placed in next line preceding branch of service

Mr. and Mrs. John William Jones
request the honour of your presence
at the marriage of their daughter
Lynn Marie
to
Ronald John Adams
First Lieutenant, United States Army

Rank below Sergeant is not indicated, branch of service is placed below name:

Mr. and Mrs. John William Jones
request the honour of your presence
at the marriage of their daughter
Lynn Marie
to
Ronald John Adams
United States Army

CONTEMPORARY WORDING

A life of sharing, caring
A love of endless giving together

Mr. and Mrs. John William Jones
request the honour of your presence
on Saturday, the second of June
Nineteen hundred and eighty-four
at seven-thirty o'clock
when their daughter
Lynn Marie
and
Ronald John Adams
become united through marriage
at American Lutheran Church
Medford, Wisconsin

• • •

In the spirit of Christian joy
Lynn Marie Jones
and Ronald John Adams
will vow their lives to one another forever
on Saturday, the second of June
Nineteen hundred and eighty-four
at seven o'clock in the evening
Their families invite you to join them
in asking God's blessing upon this holy union
American Lutheran Church
Medford, Wisconsin

• • •

A fresh new day...and it is our
a day of happy beginnings
when we, Lynn Marie Jones
and Ronald John Adams
pledge our lives as one
on Saturday, June second
Nineteen hundred and eighty-four
at seven o'clock
American Lutheran Church
Medford, Wisconsin

• • •

Lynn Marie Jones
and
Ronald John Adams
invite you to share

a day of happiness
as they begin a life of love
on Saturday, June second
at six o'clock
American Lutheran Church
Medford, Wisconsin

• • •

Believing that Holy Matrimony is ordained by God
and in the Spirit of Christian joy
Mr. and Mrs. John William Jones
request the honour of your presence
at the ceremony in which their daughter
Lynn Marie Jones
and
Ronald John Adams
will vow their lives to one another
and become united as one in Christ
Saturday, June second
Nineteen hundred and eighty-four
at one o'clock
American Lutheran Church
Medford, Wisconsin

• • •

The most joyous of occasions
is the union of man and woman
in the celebration of life...
Mr. and Mrs. John William Jones
invite you to share in the ceremony
uniting their daughter
—OR—
Lynn Marie Jones
and
Ronald John Adams
invite you to share in the joy
when they exchange marriage vows
and begin their new life together
—OR—
Lynn Marie Jones
and
Ronald John Adams

have chosen the first day
of their new life together
—OR—
Mr. and Mrs. John William Jones
and
Mr. and Mrs. Eugene Francis Adams
invite you to share in the joy of
the marriage uniting their children
Lynn Marie
and
Ronald John
This celebration of love will be
—OR—
Because you have shared in their lives
by your friendship and love
you are invited to share with
our daughter Lynn Marie
and Ronald John Adams
when they exchange marriage vows
and begin their new life together
on Saturday, June second
Nineteen hundred and eighty-four
at six o'clock
American Lutheran Church
Medford, Wisconsin
Mr. and Mrs. John William Jones
• • •
Lynn Marie Jones
and
Ronald John Adams
together with their parents
Mr. and Mrs. John William Jones
and
Mr. and Mrs. Eugene Francis Adams
invite you to share in the joy
when they exchange marriage vows
and begin their new life together

Our joy will be more complete
if you can share in the marriage
of our daughter, Lynn Marie
to Ronald John Adams
on Saturday, the second of June
Nineteen hundred and eighty-four
at seven o'clock in the evening
at American Lutheran Church
Medford, Wisconsin
We invite you
to worship with us and witness their vows
If you are unable to attend
we ask your presence in thought and prayer
Mr. and Mrs. John William Jones

• • •

With joyful hearts
we ask you to be present
at the ceremony uniting our daughter
Lynn Marie
and
Mr. Ronald John Adams
Saturday, the second of June
Nineteen hundred and eighty-four
at four o'clock
at American Lutheran Church
Medford, Wisconsin
Mr. and Mrs. John William Jones

• • •

Our daughter, Lynn Marie, and Ronald John Adams will be united in Christ on Saturday, the second of June, nineteen hundred and eighty-four at one-thirty o'clock in the afternoon at the American Lutheran Church, Medford, Wisconsin.

You are invited to join in worship, witness their vows, and celebrate their union at a reception following the ceremony in the Church Parlors.

If you are unable to attend, we ask your presence in thought and prayer.

Mr. and Mrs. John William Jones

PRINTER CHECKLIST

Printer's name: Phone#:

Address:

COST

Guaranteed rate? Deposit? Amount?

When is deposit due? When is balance due?

How does the printer bill me?

Cancellation terms:

QUANTITIES

Tissues: R.S.V.P.: Ceremony: Reception:

Thank-you notes: Napkins: Matches: Envelopes:

Ceremony programs: Reception favors: Wedding file cards:

OTHER PARTICULARS

Paper stock: Paper color:

Syle of lettering used:

Other colors used (informal only):

When will I be able to pick up my order?:

Can I pick up my envelopes early for addressing?:

What kind of a selection of wedding favors do they have?:

WORDING

Invitations: ______________________________

____

____

____

____

Ceremony program: ______________________________

____

____

____

____

____

____

____

____

R.S.V.P.: ______________________________

____

Reception cards: ______________________________

____

Matches: ______________________________

Napkins: ______________________________

____

____

____

Softly, as the colors
of a Rainbow
Our lives are touched
by Love

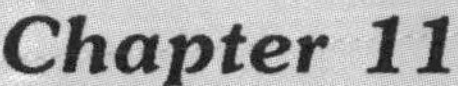

Chapter 11

Wedding Party

THE WEDDING PARTY

Early in the planning stages of your wedding, you and your fiance' should choose those special people who will be your attendants. Usually you choose your closest friends and relatives to share in the excitement of your big day. Following is a list of the traditional wedding participants and their responsibilities:

MAID OF HONOR AND/OR PERSONAL ATTENDANTS

The maid of honor is usually a special friend or sister of the bride. She is expected to help the bride as much as possible.

___ Helps the bride with addressing invitations, serves as a shopping advisor, helps bride with gifts, etc.
___ Attends all pre-wedding parties, showers, etc.
___ Pays for her own wedding attire.
___ Helps in organizing the bridesmaids and their wedding attire, and makes sure they know their ceremonial duties.
___ Is in charge of the groom's wedding ring until the appropriate time during the ceremony, when she exchanges it for the bride's bouquet.
___ Along with the best man, signs the wedding certificate as a legal witness.
___ Helps the bride in arranging her veil and train, and also when dressing for the wedding.
___ She is also a member of the receiving line.
___ Helps the bride get dressed in her going-away clothes, and takes the bridal gown to the cleaners, or to the bride's home.

BRIDESMAIDS

The bridesmaids are primarily to add a warm, personal, colorful touch to the wedding festivities. They are always invited to all pre-wedding parties, showers, etc.

___ Bridesmaids are responsible for the purchase and fitting of their wedding attire (the bride may wish to buy their accessories).
___ Bridesmaids may assist the bride with pre-wedding tasks and errands.
___ Bridesmaids participate in rehearsal and ceremony and also in the receiving line.

BEST MAN

The best man is usually a brother or best friend of the groom. He is the groom's right-hand man in organizing his activities for the day.

___ Helps to host the bachelor party (or dinner, which is optional).
___ Pays for his own wedding attire.
___ The best man transports the groom to the church, and helps him dress for the ceremony.
___ Supervises the groomsmen and ushers and makes sure they are properly dressed and that they know their duties.
___ The best man takes care of the bride's ring until the appropriate time during the ceremony.
___ He presents the clergyperson with his/her fee either just before or just after the ceremony.
___ The best man, along with the maid of honor, signs the wedding certificate as a legal witness.
___ The best man offers the first toast to the bride and groom at the reception, and reads aloud any congratulatory telegrams.
___ The best man dances with the bride after the groom and both fathers have danced with her.
___ Makes sure that the honeymoon car is ready and the suitcases are packed and put in the car.
___ He helps the groom get into his travelling clothes—takes care of any tickets, keys, etc. given to him for safekeeping.
___ He transports the newlyweds to the airport or from wherever they are leaving for their honeymoon.
___ The best man returns the groom's formal wear either to his home or back to the formal wear shop.

GROOMSMEN

The groomsmen are usually close friends, brothers, or relatives of the couple.

___ They pay for their own wedding attire.
___ They attend the bachelor dinner or party (if one is held).
___ They attend the rehearsal and rehearsal dinner.
___ They escort the bridesmaids during the ceremony processional and recessional.

USHERS

Ushers have more details to attend to. They should be specifically instructed as to their responsibilities.

___ They pay for their own wedding attire.
___ They should arrive at the church at least an hour before the ceremony.
___ They light the candles about 15 minutes before the ceremony begins (if this assignment is given to them by the clergy).
___ The ushers should obtain from the couple a list of guests for special or reserved seating.
___ They should make sure that grandparents, godparents, etc. have their flowers before they are seated.
___ The ushers distribute wedding service programs to the guests while seating them; or they may put the programs in the pews ahead of time.
___ The usher should introduce himself/herself to the guest and should ask whether he/she is a guest of the bride or the groom.
___ The bride's guests are traditionally seated on the left side and the groom's guests seated on the right side. Sides are reversed in an Orthodox Jewish wedding. Ushers may choose to balance the sides if one is filling up much faster than the other. In many church weddings, parents now go down the aisle with their respective children.
___ The usher should offer his/her right arm to the woman of a pair of guests, or to the oldest woman of a group. Other members of the guest group walk slightly behind as the usher escorts them to their seats. Single men may simply walk beside the usher.
___ The groom's parents should be seated last of all. They should be seated in the right front pew, and then the bride's mother in the left front pew. After the head usher escorts the bride's mother to her seat, no more guests are seated until after the processional. In some cases, the families are just simply seated as they come in.
___ After carefully unrolling the aisle carpet, the ushers should take their places. An extra usher should remain to seat latecomers.

___ The ushers should escort the parents of the bridal couple and any special designated guests out of the church after the recessional.

___ The ushers then indicate to other guests pew by pew, when they may leave their seats following the recessional.

___ Check over the church/synagogue to see that it is left clean and orderly.

MOTHER OF THE BRIDE

___ Assists the bride in selecting gown and accessories, wedding colors and attendant's attire, and personal trousseau.

___ Helps in compiling the guest list, and in addressing invitations.

___ Provides friends with information about gift registry preferences of the bride.

___ Assists in ceremony and reception details.

___ Selects her own dress and consults with the groom's mother on their styles and colors of dresses.

___ Keeps the father of the bride and the groom's parents informed on wedding plans and preparations.

___ May take care of incoming gifts.

___ Acts as the official hostess at the wedding and reception. She is the last person to be seated at the ceremony and the first to greet the guests in the receiving line. (See previous usher section.) The bride's mother also sits in the place of honor at the parents' table. However, this is at the discretion of the bride and her mother.

___ May ride with father of the bride to the ceremony or assist in dressing the bride the day of the ceremony.

FATHER OF THE BRIDE

___ Rides with the bride to the ceremony.

___ In the traditional procession, he escorts his daughter during the processional, then sits with the mother of the bride in the left front pew. However, many brides walk down the aisle with both parents. (See also groom's parents.)

___ Preferably stands in the receiving line or may mingle as the host of the reception.

___ The father of the bride should dress in conformance with the groom and his attendants.

___ The father of the bride is usually the last person to leave the reception, and also bids guests farewell.

GROOM'S PARENTS

___ The groom's parents should call on the bride's parents to express their approval as soon as possible after the engagement.
___ The groom's parents might walk down the aisle with their son.
___ The groom's parents sit in the right front pew during the ceremony and they are special guests at the reception.
___ The groom's mother always stands in the receiving line, and the father may stand in the receiving line or mingle with the crowd.

FLOWER GIRL AND /OR RING BEARER

* Note—Decisions relative to the use of flower girl and/or ring bearer have become a delicate one to make; in fact, many churches are discouraging this practice of rather dubious "origins."

___ The flower girl is usually between the ages of 4 and 10. Her dress may be exactly like the bridesmaids' or something similar. She should carry a small bouquet, or basket. She precedes the bride and her father.
___ The ring bearer is usually between the ages of 3 and 6 years of age. He carries a small pillow with a ring stitched onto it (preferably a fake ring). He also precedes the bride and her father.
___ The ring bearer may be dressed in short white pants, with a fancy white shirt, bow tie, and white shoes; or he may be dressed to match the men in the wedding party.
___ The parents of the flower girl and ring bearer pay for their children's wedding attire.
___ The flower girl and ring bearer should be included in transportation arrangements.
___ The children and their parents should be included in the rehearsal and rehearsal dinner.
___ The children do not have to stand in the receiving line.
___ It is a wise suggestion to have a babysitter to take care of the children during the reception so that the parents can relax and enjoy the evening.

OTHER PARTICIPANTS

You may find that you would like more friends and relatives involved than the size of your wedding party allows. There are a number of other duties that need attention. You might have a friend read a scripture passage at the ceremony; or serve as a candlelighter; or greet guests as they arrive.

You may need assistance at the reception also. You could possibly ask a group of friends, or relatives, to decorate the hall, and to be in charge of the wedding gifts—take them either to your parents' home or your new home. You might ask younger cousins or friends to attend the guest book, serve punch and coffee, and clean up after the reception.

With an endless love
we'll share our thoughts,
our dreams, ourselves.

NOTES

____

____

____

____

____

____

____

____

____

____

____

____

____

NOTES

Our love,
shining like the dawn,
beautiful as the moon,
radiant as the sun

Chapter 12

Wedding Attire

WEDDING ATTIRE

Bridal gowns, like other wedding customs, are wide open to personal preference. There are so many styles and fabrics to choose from! The choice is yours completely. Take the time to look through bridal magazines to get some idea of what you would like. There will be a wedding dress perfect for you no matter what style or tone you want to set for your wedding.

There are a number of things to consider when choosing your wedding dress:

* The size and type of wedding you want: For a formal wedding, white or ivory is traditional with a long dress in any elegant fabric and a headpiece with a veil. For a semi-formal wedding your choices are the same, but not quite as formal. For an informal wedding you may choose whatever is tasteful and becoming to you. Headpieces should be coordinated with whatever dress you choose.
* Also keep in mind the season of the year—you will want to wear fabrics that are comfortable and appropriate. Basically, there are two design seasons—spring/summer and fall/winter.
* Choose a dress that is becoming to your figure, height and taste. Take the time to note the full effect of a dress, since your guests will see more of the back of you than the front during the ceremony.
* Consider the budget with which you are working. Of course, you want the gown of your dreams, but be down-to-earth on the maximum amount you can afford to spend. When going to the bridal shops, inform the consultant of your price range, which will provide a guideline as to which dresses to show you.
* Shop for your dress at least six months in advance of the wedding date. Most dresses have to be special-ordered, and you may need to have alterations made. This will also ensure that your dress arrives in time for the wedding!
* When going for fittings, wear the undergarments, shoes, and accessories that you plan to wear on your wedding day.
* Accessories should be kept to a minimum. Perhaps a pair of small earrings or a necklace of gold or pearls would give the finishing touch to your appearance.
* Most shops require a deposit when you place your order. Payment and cancellation policies vary, so inquire beforehand. Some allow a five-day cancellation period; others place the

order immediately, which means you must forfeit your deposit and pay for the dress. Keep all slips. Be sure everything promised is in writing and read the sales agreement carefully. The delivery date of the dress and headpiece should also be included.

If you allow enough time to shop for your dress, and work closely with the bridal shop consultant, you'll find the dress that's uniquely you!

The following is a guideline to help you better understand "bridal shop talk" when shopping for your wedding attire.

SLEEVES

* Bishop—fuller in the lower forearm, then gathered at wrist into a wide cuff.
* Dolman—extending from an armhole so large it creates a cape-like effect, often fitted at the wrist.
* Leg-of-mutton (or Gigot)—full, loose, rounded from shoulder to slightly below elbow, then nipped in at wrist.
* Melon—extravagantly rounded from shoulder to elbow.
* Puff—gathered into gentle puff near shoulders.

SILHOUETTES

* Ballgown—appealing, off-the-shoulder yoke nipping into a natural waist with lavish, full skirt.
* Basque—natural waist with V-front and a full skirt.
* Empire—small, scooped bodice gathering at high waist, a slim yet full skirt.
* Princess—slim-fitting style, with vertical seams flowing from shoulders down to hem of flared skirt.
* Sheath—narrow, body-hugging style without a waist.

LENGTHS OF DRESSES AND TRAINS

* Street Length—hem just covering knees.
* Intermission Length—hem falling slightly below or mid-way between the knee and ankle.
* Ballet Length—hem swirling to ankles.
* Floor Length—hem fully skimming the floor.
* Sweep Train—shortest train, barely sweeping the floor.

* Court Train—a train extending one foot longer than the sweep train.
* Chapel Train—most popular of all bridal trains—trailing about 1-1/3 yards from waist.
* Cathedral Train—worn at a very formal wedding—tumbling 2-1/2 yards from waist.
* Extended Cathedral Train, unfolding 3 yards from waist.

NECKLINES

* High—collar just brushing the chin.
* Off-the-shoulder—gracefully hovering above bustline, sometimes attached to a sheer net yoke and high collar.
* Boat or Bateau—gently following curve of the collarbone—high in front and back, opening wide at sides, ending in shoulder seams.
* Queen Anne—rising high at the nape (back) of neck, then sculpting low to outline a bare yoke.
* Square—shaped like half of a square.
* Sweetheart—shaped like the top half of a heart.

FABRICS

* Brocade—heavy fabric with interwoven, raised design.
* Chiffon—delicately sheer, a simple weaving—often of silk or rayon—with a soft or stiff finishing.
* Eyelet—open-weave embroidery used for decorations.
* Moire—silk taffeta that, when illuminated, glistens like water.
* Organza—sheer, crisply textured fabric, almost transparent.
* Silk-faced Satin—brimming with body, with a dusty sheen.
* Slipper Satin—light, soft—a more closely woven fabric.
* Taffeta—smooth, glossy—a finely textured fabric with body.
* Tulle—tiny-meshed net of silk, cotton, or synthetics.
* Polyester may also be used for dresses, alone or blended with natural fibers, like polyorganza or polychiffon.

HEADPIECES

* Coronet—wreath resting high on crown of the head.
* Floral Wreath—circlet of flowers which can nestle on top of the head or at mid-forehead.
* Half Hat—small hat covering half, or less than half, of crown.

* Juliet Cap—small cap, ornately festooned with pearls and jewels, that snugly hugs the crown.
* Mantilla—lace-trimmed netting usually secured to an elegant comb, gently framing the face.
* Picture Hat—ornamented hat with a very large brim.
* Tiara—crown, usually encrusted with crystals, pearls, or lace, resting high atop the head.
* Toque—small, close-fitting hat without a brim.
* Upturned Picture Hat—picture hat with brim tilting up to one side.
* Except for the Mantilla, veiling is usually attached to all of these headpieces.

LACE

* Alençon—originated in Alençon, France—a pretty, delicate, yet durable design, outlined with cord on net ground.
* Chantilly—from Chantilly, France—graceful, floral sprays on fine lace background, outlined with silk threads.
* Schiffli—machine-made, delicate floral embroidery.
* Venice—heavy, raised, floral design, first made in Venice.

VEILS

* Blusher—loose veil worn forward over face or back over the headpiece, often attached to longer, three-tiered veil.
* Fly-away—multi-layers that brush the shoulders, usually worn with an informal, ankle-length dress or a style with too-pretty-to-hide details in back.
* Birdcage—falling just below chin, gently shirred at the sides, and usually attached to hats.
* Chapel Length—tumbling 2-1/3 yards from headpiece.
* Cathedral Length—cascading 3-1/2 yards from headpiece, usually worn with cathedral train.
* Ballet or Waltz Length—falling to the ankles.
* Fingertip—most popular length, gracefully touching the fingertips.
* Most veils are made of nylon material called illusion. Decorations often include poufs, which are small gathers of veiling on the crown of a headpiece. Wreaths often have flowing ribbons called streamers, tied into "love knots."

Once you have selected your dress, you should choose the attire for your attendants. Their dresses should compliment your dress. For a formal wedding their dresses should be floor length; at a less formal wedding, they can be shorter, even if your dress is long. Again, keep in mind their height, weight, and coloring. Also keep in mind their budgets since they will be paying for their own dresses. Shoes should be comfortable, and should preferably be dyed to match the dresses.

Both mothers should wear a dress appropriate for the style and formality of your wedding. Let them talk it over between themselves and with your assistance they will be able to select dresses that will be becoming and compatible.

The wedding attire of the groom, as well as that of the other men in the bridal party should complement the attire of the bride and her attendants with respect to the degree of formality and the time of day for the wedding ceremony. Traditionally, the groom, best man, groomsmen, ushers and both fathers dress alike, except that subtle differences in their accessories—the style of shirt, collar, tie, etc., differentiate the groom and possibly the best man from the other men. Coordinating or matching attire should be worn by the ring bearer, if there is one.

Again, looking through bridal magazines will help you get some ideas as to styles available. Plan to visit the formal wear store at least six weeks in advance of the wedding date. Take sample swatches of the bridesmaid's dresses with you to help coordinate colors. Once you have selected the men's formal wear, you will need to make arrangements for the men to have their measurements taken and formal wear fitted.

If you have any questions concerning the style or formality of the wedding clothes, ask your bridal shop representative or formal wear specialist. They will be able to answer any questions you may have and will be able to assist you in choosing the appropriate style for the type of wedding you have chosen.

NOTES

___

___

___

WEDDING ATTIRE CHECKLIST

BRIDAL SHOP: ____________________ PHONE: ______

ADDRESS: ______________________________________

REPRESENTATIVE: ________________________________

BRIDE'S DRESS

STYLE: ______________________ COLOR: _________

______________________________ SIZE: __________

HEADPIECE: __________________ COLOR: _________

UNDERGARMENTS: ___________ SHOES: _________

FITTING DATES: ______________ TIME: ___________

______________ TIME: ___________

PICK UP DATES: ______________ COST: ___________

PAYMENT RECORD

DATE: _______ AMOUNT: _______ BALANCE: _______

DATE: _______ AMOUNT: _______ BALANCE: _______

DATE: _______ AMOUNT: _______ BALANCE: _______

DATE: _______ AMOUNT: _______ BALANCE: _______

NOTES

____

____

____

____

ATTENDANTS

STYLE: ______________________ COLOR: __________

______________________ SIZE: __________

HEADPIECE: ______________________ COLOR: __________

UNDERGARMENTS: ______________ SHOES: __________

FITTING DATES: ______________ TIME: __________

______________ TIME: __________

PICK UP DATES: ______________ COST: __________

PAYMENT RECORD

DATE: ________ AMOUNT: ________ BALANCE: ________

DATE: ________ AMOUNT: ________ BALANCE: ________

DATE: ________ AMOUNT: ________ BALANCE: ________

DATE: ________ AMOUNT: ________ BALANCE: ________

NAME: ______________________ PHONE#: __________

ADDRESS: ______________________________________

NOTES

____

____

____

____

____

____

ATTENDANTS

STYLE: ______________________ COLOR: __________
______________________ SIZE: __________
HEADPIECE: ______________________ COLOR: __________
UNDERGARMENTS: __________ SHOES: __________
FITTING DATES: ______________ TIME: __________
______________ TIME: __________
PICK UP DATES: ______________ COST: __________

PAYMENT RECORD

DATE: ________ AMOUNT: ________ BALANCE: ________
DATE: ________ AMOUNT: ________ BALANCE: ________
DATE: ________ AMOUNT: ________ BALANCE: ________
DATE: ________ AMOUNT: ________ BALANCE: ________

NAME: ______________________ PHONE#: __________
ADDRESS: ______________________________________

NOTES

____
____
____
____
____
____

ATTENDANTS

STYLE:______________________________ COLOR: ____________

______________________________ SIZE: ______________

HEADPIECE:_______________________ COLOR: ____________

UNDERGARMENTS: _______________ SHOES: ____________

FITTING DATES: __________________ TIME:_______________

__________________ TIME:_______________

PICK UP DATES: _________________ COST:______________

PAYMENT RECORD

DATE:_________ AMOUNT:_________ BALANCE: _________

DATE:_________ AMOUNT:_________ BALANCE: _________

DATE:_________ AMOUNT:_________ BALANCE: _________

DATE:_________ AMOUNT:_________ BALANCE: _________

NAME: _________________________ PHONE#: ______________

ADDRESS: ____

NOTES

____

____

____

____

____

____

ATTENDANTS

STYLE: ____________ COLOR: ____________
____________ SIZE: ____________
HEADPIECE: ____________ COLOR: ____________
UNDERGARMENTS: ____________ SHOES: ____________
FITTING DATES: ____________ TIME: ____________
____________ TIME: ____________
PICK UP DATES: ____________ COST: ____________

PAYMENT RECORD

DATE: ________ AMOUNT: ________ BALANCE: ________
DATE: ________ AMOUNT: ________ BALANCE: ________
DATE: ________ AMOUNT: ________ BALANCE: ________
DATE: ________ AMOUNT: ________ BALANCE: ________

NAME: ____________ PHONE#: ____________
ADDRESS: ____________

NOTES

____
____
____
____
____
____

MOTHER OF THE BRIDE

STYLE:______________________ COLOR: __________
______________________ SIZE: __________
FITTING DATES: ______________ TIME: __________
______________ TIME: __________
PICK UP DATES: ______________ COST: __________

MOTHER OF THE GROOM

STYLE:______________________ COLOR: __________
______________________ SIZE: __________
FITTING DATES: ______________ TIME: __________
______________ TIME: __________
PICK UP DATES: ______________ COST: __________

FORMAL WEAR SHOP:__________ PHONE: __________
ADDRESS: ______________________________
REPRESENTATIVE: ______________________________

NOTES

____

____

____

____

GROOM'S TUXEDO

STYLE: ____________________ COLOR: __________

____________________ SIZE: __________

PACKAGE INCLUDES: ____________________

FITTING DATES: ____________________ TIME: __________

____________________ TIME: __________

PICK UP DATES: ____________________ COST: __________

FATHER OF THE BRIDE

STYLE: ____________________ COLOR: __________

____________________ SIZE: __________

PACKAGE INCLUDES: ____________________

FITTING DATES: ____________________ TIME: __________

____________________ TIME: __________

PICK UP DATES: ____________________ COST: __________

FATHER OF THE GROOM

STYLE: ____________________ COLOR: __________

____________________ SIZE: __________

PACKAGE INCLUDES: ____________________

FITTING DATES: ____________________ TIME: __________

____________________ TIME: __________

PICK UP DATES: ____________________ COST: __________

NOTES

____

____

GROOMSMEN/USHERS

STYLE:______________________________ COLOR: ____________
______________________________ SIZE: ______________
PACKAGE INCLUDES: ______________________________________
FITTING DATES: ____________________ TIME: ______________
____________________ TIME: ______________
PICK UP DATES: ___________________ COST: ______________
FORMAL WEAR MUST BE RETURNED BY: ______________

NAME: ___________________________ PHONE#: _____________
ADDRESS: ____

GROOMSMEN/USHERS

STYLE:______________________________ COLOR: ____________
______________________________ SIZE: ______________
PACKAGE INCLUDES: ______________________________________
FITTING DATES: ____________________ TIME: ______________
____________________ TIME: ______________
PICK UP DATES: ___________________ COST: ______________
FORMAL WEAR MUST BE RETURNED BY: ______________

NAME: ___________________________ PHONE#: _____________
ADDRESS: ____

NOTES

____

____

GROOMSMEN/USHERS

STYLE: ______________________ COLOR: __________

______________________ SIZE: __________

PACKAGE INCLUDES: ______________________

FITTING DATES: ______________ TIME: __________

______________ TIME: __________

PICK UP DATES: ______________ COST: __________

FORMAL WEAR MUST BE RETURNED BY: __________

NAME: ______________________ PHONE#: __________
ADDRESS: ______________________

GROOMSMEN/USHERS

STYLE: ______________________ COLOR: __________

______________________ SIZE: __________

PACKAGE INCLUDES: ______________________

FITTING DATES: ______________ TIME: __________

______________ TIME: __________

PICK UP DATES: ______________ COST: __________

FORMAL WEAR MUST BE RETURNED BY: __________

NAME: ______________________ PHONE#: __________
ADDRESS: ______________________

NOTES

____

____

Last Minute Fix-Up Kit

It is a good suggestion to have a handy "first aid" kit with you (or your mother) on your wedding day. A ripped hem or seam, snagged panty hose, unruly hair, etc., are problems no bride wants to put up with on her wedding day. A handy little kit—perhaps a decorated shoe box, or sewing kit—should be with the bridal party at all times. You may wish to leave it in the lady's restroom at the place of your reception, as long as it is not a **public** restroom. Items to include are:

Safety pins
Band-Aids
Hair pins
Tissues
Breath mints
Hand towelettes
Nail polish
Scissors
Needle and thread to match dresses
Comb/brush
Baby powder
Scotch tape
Nail file
Tampons
Aspirin
Pantyhose
Mascara
Lip gloss
Contact lens fluid
Hair spray
Blush
And any other items you may feel necessary to have around on your big day!

In your heart
is my heart locked
and in your life,
my life

To have and
to hold from
this day forward,
for better, for worse
in sickness and in health,
to love and to cherish,
'till death us
do part.

Chapter 13

Ceremony Planning

CEREMONY PLANNING

First of all, you will have to decide on what type of wedding you want to have. This will depend on the amount of money you want to spend, the number of guests you want to invite, where and when your ceremony and reception will be held, and the degree of formality you want your wedding to express.

A FORMAL wedding means that you basically want to conform to strict traditional marriage rites both of the church and of secular society. Generally, a formal wedding is larger both in size of wedding party and number of guests invited, and features more elaborate decorations, attire, invitations, and reception arrangements, than a semi-formal or informal wedding.

SEMI-FORMAL weddings basically stay with tradition, but everything is slightly less elaborate and more flexible than a formal wedding. Semi-formal weddings may take place in a church, a club, or a hotel.

An INFORMAL wedding can be either a simple ceremony or you can let your imagination go to work. Informal weddings normally have a smaller wedding party and fewer guests than formal or semi-formal weddings.

If you plan on a church wedding, you should make an appointment to meet with your clergyperson as soon as possible after you set your wedding date. He/she will be able to advise you on any pre-marital requirements, such as counseling, that the church may require. He/she can also answer any questions you may have concerning the ceremony itself. He/she can guide you in the selection of music, any church wedding customs, and help you with special vows or other liturgical elements you would like to have in your wedding service. He will also be able to tell you if there are any restrictions concerning church flowers, photography, fire laws, church capacity, availability of kneelers and other equipment, and dressing facilities for attendants.

If you are planning to have a civil ceremony, you should talk to the justice of the peace or judge who will marry you to set a date, time, and place for the ceremony. Usually, only the immediate family and a few guests attend.

You may decide to have your wedding ceremony in a hotel or club, with either a civil or religious person officiating. Keep in mind that many of the items you will need may not be supplied, so you will have to rent them. Check with the hotel to see which items are available.

A home wedding can be formal or informal. Keep in mind the number of guests that your home can comfortably accommodate. Don't move all the furniture out just to make more room or you will lose the "homey" atmosphere you wanted in the first place.

If you plan an outdoor ceremony, keep in mind that the weather may not always cooperate and have an alternate location readily available. Try to pick a quiet spot without much traffic, general outdoor noise, etc.

If you plan to have your wedding ceremony take place in a location other than a church, keep in mind the preparations you will have to make. Things to consider are how accessible the site is, what facilities exist for guest parking and seating, and what equipment is available.

When determining the date and time of your wedding, your work/school schedule, convenience for families, and your honeymoon plans should be taken into consideration. Saturday is usually the day chosen for weddings, but any day is acceptable. In fact, many weddings are being held on Friday evenings due to most people's schedules and the availability of reception halls.

Everything must be rehearsed. The only way to be sure all goes well is to rehearse the ceremony. Everyone must attend. It is helpful for all of the attendants to hear the processional and recessional music so the pace of their step can be timed. The ushers should also be briefed on their duties. The entire wedding party should become familiar with the church/synogogue/temple. This includes the interior, exits, vestry, waiting room, and dressing room if neccessary.

The wedding rehearsal should be scheduled for the evening before. Allow at least 2 hours. The rehearsal should be pleasant and fun. This will allow you a sense of relief in knowing everyone is well informed.

A rehearsal dinner generally follows immediately afterwards, and is traditionally paid for by the groom or his family. Be sure to keep it an early evening, however. Tomorrow, the day of your wedding, requires you to be alert and cheerful.

THOUGHTS ON THE JEWISH WEDDING

"There is no such thing as a 'generic' Jewish wedding—no matter what the rabbi tells you, no matter what your mother tells you, no matter what the caterer tells you."

Anita Diamant,
from *The Jewish Wedding*

AMERICA THE PLURAL

America is a land of many religions. It must also be said that America is a land where there is a diversity of practice within religious communities. Judaism is no exception.

MAKE FRIENDS WITH A RABBI

In today's mobile society, many people are not in a position to avail themselves of a "family rabbi". Finding a rabbi is not as difficult as one might think. Wherever there is at least one synagogue, the local rabbi, cantor or administrator can help you.

The most important thing is finding a rabbi with whom you can be comfortable.This will depend on the rabbi's role in your marriage plans.

If you want a simple marriage facilitator, that is one thing. But if you want your rabbi to be more than an agent of civil and religious authority with whom you have an impersonal relationship, you must look for a good fit.

A rabbi should be able to advise you on any facet of your wedding plans, even if you are looking for a calligrapher, caterer, or musician. Most importantly, your rabbi can be a guide in the establishment of the new "house" within the people Israel, with all the religious, ethnic and sociological aspects this entails.

BEWARE OF LABELS

Rabbis should be chosen on the basis of expertise and sensitivity. There are many fine rabbis who serve in different branches of the Jewish faith. Choose a rabbi, not a label.

WORKING WITH YOUR RABBI

No subject you wish to discuss is taboo. Your rabbi, however, will be most concerned with the following:

1. Are both marriage partners born of Jewish mothers or properly converted to Judaism?
2. In case of a second marriage, the rabbi will want to know if a proper religious divorce has nullified the marriage.
3. Some rabbis will want to know if the marriage is of a type prohibited by Jewish Law.
4. The rabbi will want to advise the couple on acceptable wedding dates. Besides the Sabbath, fast days, and holy days, there are approximately 10 weeks on the calendar when it is traditional not to marry (approximately mid-April to early June, and late July).

Note—Many rabbis will not take part in an inter-faith marriage ceremony. This is not to be taken personally. Intermarriage is not recognized in traditional circles.

A JEWISH WEDDING LIST

Jewish weddings can be held anywhere a simple Huppah (canopy) can be set up. Generally, the wedding is held where the reception/feast will follow. In addition, the following ceremonial items need to be provided:

A drawn, witnessed marriage contract
Two witnesses recognized by Jewish Law
Two wine goblets
Kosher wine
A carefully wrapped glass (the groom will smash it with his left foot at the end of the ceremony.)
A single, plain wedding band (which the groom will present to the bride in the course of the ceremony.)
Enough skullcaps (Kippot) for the men in the wedding party and invited guests.

Note—Double ring ceremonies are not recognized in traditional circles. In all cases, do not be afraid to ask the rabbi what they will permit.

THE JEWISH WEDDING IN ACTION

(See traditional formation diagram on the following page.)

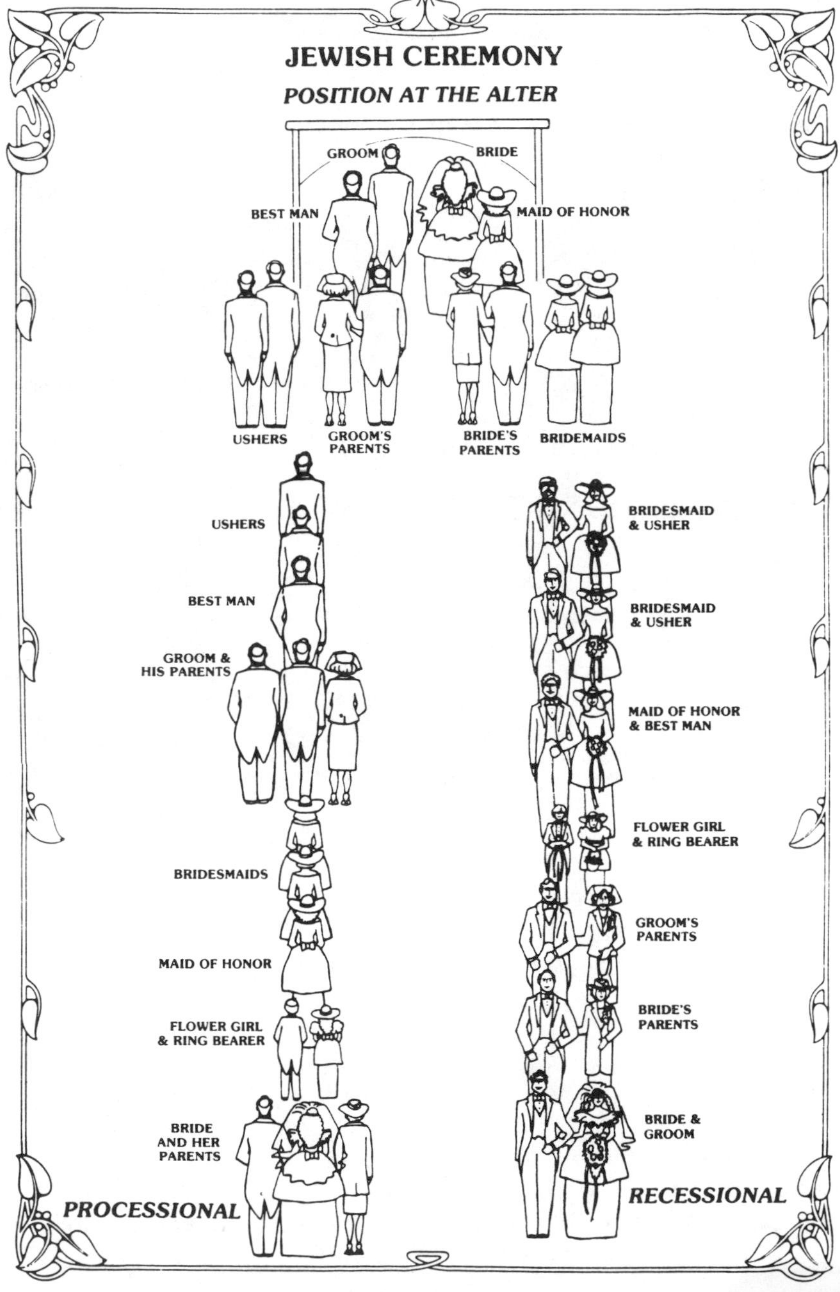
JEWISH CEREMONY
POSITION AT THE ALTER
GROOM
BRIDE
BEST MAN
MAID OF HONOR
USHERS
GROOM'S PARENTS
BRIDE'S PARENTS
BRIDEMAIDS
USHERS
BEST MAN
GROOM & HIS PARENTS
BRIDESMAIDS
MAID OF HONOR
FLOWER GIRL & RING BEARER
BRIDE AND HER PARENTS
PROCESSIONAL
BRIDESMAID & USHER
BRIDESMAID & USHER
MAID OF HONOR & BEST MAN
FLOWER GIRL & RING BEARER
GROOM'S PARENTS
BRIDE'S PARENTS
BRIDE & GROOM
RECESSIONAL

You may choose to have a rabbi/cantor duo performing your wedding, where the cantor chants the wedding blessings. You may also divide the service between two rabbis.

The wedding procession makes its way to the canopy where the rabbi usually waits. Processional music is not a religious requirement.

It is beautiful to have family and attendants standing at the side of the canopy. This intimacy and sense of community goes hand in hand with the "new house" that is being established under the wedding canopy.

In very traditional weddings, the bride circles her groom seven times as both mothers hold the train of her dress. In Hebrew Scripture it is written, "And when a man takes a wife" seven times. It is a beautiful touch.

THE WEDDING CEREMONY

The blessing of betrothal are recited, followed by a sip from the first cup of wine. Many holy acts in the Jewish faith are consecrated over wine.

The groom presents a plain ring to his bride and makes the following declaration:

"Be betrothed to me with this ring according to the law of Moses and Israel."

In accepting this simple item of recognizable value in the presence of witnesses, the bride is betrothed to her husband. After the ceremony a more elaborate ring can be substituted.

Now the Ketubah (marriage contract certificate) is read aloud. In it, a couple's mutual obligations under Jewish law are spelled out. It is signed by witnesses and not by the couple themselves. The rabbi then delivers his message and personal blessing to the couple.

The ceremony concludes with the recitation of seven wedding benedictions, a sip from the second cup of wine and the breaking of a glass. The reason for this custom is based on the belief that as long as the world is not redeemed, there cannot be total joy. The shattering of glass is a recognition of the imperfection that exists in the world. It is also a symbol of our lives. Life is fragile like glass and whatever time is alloted to us must be used well.

With the ceremony now complete, all somberness is banished from thought. On with the festivities!

WHO PAYS?

In the "good old days" the bride's family assumed all costs except the liquor, flowers and photography. Today, expenses are often negotiated.

INVITATIONS

Inclusion of both sets of parents names is standard. Often a facing page of Hebrew translation is incorporated. This requires a calligrapher or a printer with typesetting capabilities.

JEWISH SOURCES

How-To Books

Diamant, Anita. *The Jewish Wedding*. New York: Summit Books, 1985.

Siegel, Richard, Strassfeld, Sharon & Michael, Editors. *The First Jewish Catalogue*. Philadelphia: The Jewish Publication Society of America, 1973.

Directories Of Goods & Services For The American Jewish Community

Strassfeld, Sharon & Michael, Editors. *The Second Jewish Catalogue*. Philadelphia: The Jewish Publication Society of America, 1976. (Features "Yellow Pages" which are periodically updated.)

Tillem, Ivan, Editor. *The Jewish Directory and Almanac*. New York: Pacific Press, 1986.

Music Sources (send for catalogues)

Velvel Pasternak
Tara Publications
29 Derby Ave.
Cedarhurst, NY 11516

Transcontinental Music Publications
838 5th Avenue
New York, NY 10021

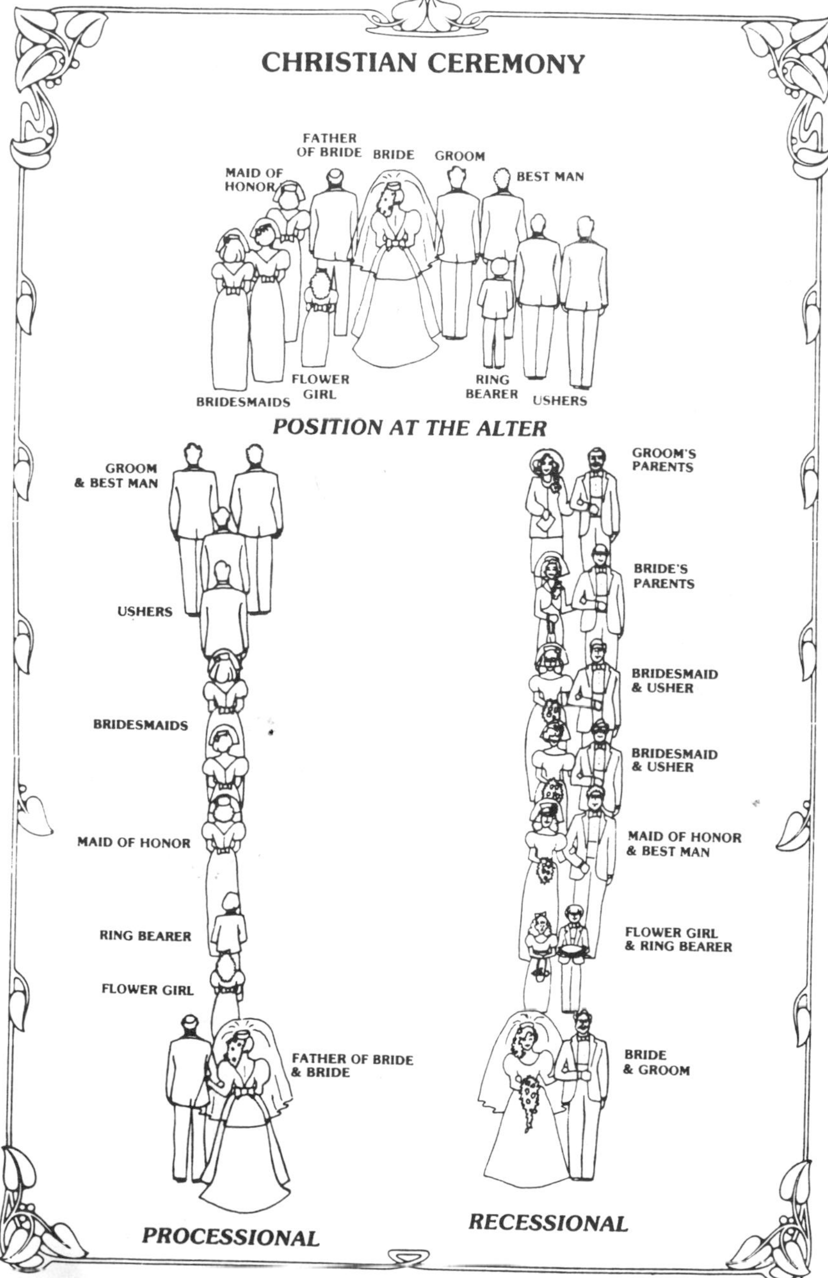
CHRISTIAN CEREMONY
FATHER OF BRIDE
BRIDE
GROOM
MAID OF HONOR
BEST MAN
FLOWER GIRL
RING BEARER
BRIDESMAIDS
USHERS
POSITION AT THE ALTER
GROOM & BEST MAN
USHERS
BRIDESMAIDS
MAID OF HONOR
RING BEARER
FLOWER GIRL
FATHER OF BRIDE & BRIDE
PROCESSIONAL
GROOM'S PARENTS
BRIDE'S PARENTS
BRIDESMAID & USHER
BRIDESMAID & USHER
MAID OF HONOR & BEST MAN
FLOWER GIRL & RING BEARER
BRIDE & GROOM
RECESSIONAL

Date and time of wedding: ____________________

Location of ceremony: ____________________

Clergymember or officiator: ____________________

Address: ____________________ Phone: ____________

Date and time of rehearsal: ____________________

Dressing facilities for bridal party: ____________________

Church requirements for:

Attire: ____________________

Flowers or decorations: ____________________

Photographer: ____________________

Type of music: ____________________

Type of readings: ____________________

Throwing of rice: ____________________

Composing own vows: ____________________

Aisle runner: ____________________

Does the church provide:

Aisle runner: ____________________

Knee cushion: ____________________

Canopy: ____________________

Officiator fees: ____________________

Organist fees: ____________________

NOTES

____

____

____

MUSIC

Music is a very important part of your wedding ceremony. **Before selecting your service music it is advisable to check with your clergyperson and organist** on any special rules for music selection that your church may have. Following is a list of suggestions for selecting your wedding music:

1. Meet with the organist before you begin selecting your music. Keep in mind that some churches have very firm guidelines on what music is used in liturgical settings. The organist should be well qualified to aid you in selecting your music.
2. Music is a service rendered as are flowers and photographs. Be sure to discuss the musicians' fees. They are generally commensurate with the performance experience, number of rehearsals and amount of music to be performed. Do not assume a friend will perform for free.
3. If at all possible, bring a musician with you when you select your music. It will enable the musician to play through any music with which you may not be familiar.
4. Know your musicians' vocal ranges and musical abilities and keep these in mind when choosing your music. (For example, most popular music comes in only one range and has only piano accompaniment available.)
5. To be sure you are ordering the correct music, know the exact title, the composer and/or arranger, the voice range, and the type of accompaniment needed. If possible, know the publisher also—which is included in the wedding music list contained in this chapter. In many cases, the musicians may want to order their own music.
6. Be sure to get enough copies of each piece. Xeroxing music is illegal and your church could get in trouble for permitting you to use copies. Most professional church organists maintain libraries of music.
7. Select your music as soon as possible. If something needs to be backordered for you it can take up to six weeks to obtain. Also, you should allow time for your musicians to familiarize themselves with the music.

8. The soloists—vocal and instrumental—should rehearse with the organist before the wedding is to take place.
9. It is nice to take the time with your family to discuss your music selections so that they understand the Church's music policies and ritual requirements. It is not a good idea to surprise them with something that may be disappointing. It is also quite possible that a family "favorite" may be inappropriate for what the Church believes is a sacred moment.
10. Always have alternate choices. Many times a song may only be available in a collection, or a particular arrangement may have gone out of print, or if you have not allowed yourself enough time, an item may be out of stock. And again, a song may be judged inappropriate in a sacramental celebration. Keep yourself open to new suggestions.

Prelude music can begin about a half hour before the ceremony begins. In a church wedding, these pieces are usually classical organ music, though other instruments such as guitars, flutes, and pianos are sometimes used. Again, consult your musician or clergyperson for suggestions.

If you are having a soloist, the time immediately before the processional is an excellent time for a song. Other songs may be sung during the service if the church customs permit.

The processional music should be majestic and joyful.

The recessional music can have much the same "presence" as the processional, but should be a slightly faster tempo with a hint of excitement.

PROCESSIONALS AND RECESSIONALS

A Wedding Processional	Near	Gray
Aginecourt Hymn	Dunstable	Presser in *Treasury Of Organ Music* ed. Biggs
Bridal Chorus (from Lohengrin)	Wagner	G. Schirmer, Belwin, and other wedding books

Cortege	Young	*Young, 11*
Organ		*Pieces*, Flammer
Epithalame (Sortie)	Willan	Berandol, BMI Canada
Epithalame (Rise Up, My Love)	Willan	Oxford
Fanfare and Processional	Wagner	Flammer
Festival Flourish	Jacob	Oxford, *Album Of Praise*
Hornpipe (from "Suite From Water Music")	Handel	J. Fischer, Novello—*Wedding Album*
Jesu, Joy Of Man's Desiring	Bach	Concordia, Oxford, etc.
Joyful, Joyful We Adore Thee	Beethoven	Hope, *Everything For The*
Wedding		
		Organist
Largo (from Xerxes)	Handel	Lorenz, *Handel Made Practical For The Church Organist*
My Spirit Be Joyful	Bach	Presser, Belwin
National hymn	Warren	Hymnals
Now Thank We All Our God	Bach	Belwin, others
Now Thank We All Our God	Johnson	Augsburg
Organ Processional For Manuals	Bender	Concordia
Praise My Soul, The King Of Heaven	Goss	Hymnals
Praise To The Lord	Manz	Concordia, *Choral Improvisations Set II*
Prelude In Classic Style	Young	Lorenz
Processional of Joy (Beethoven's Ninth Symphony)	Beethoven	C. Fischer
Procession On "Westminster Abbey"	Wetzler	Concordia
Rigaudon	Campra	Belwin
Saint Anthony Chorale	Hayden	Hymnals
Thanks Be To Thee (Arioso)	Handel	Hymnals
Triumphal March	Grieg	Peters
Toccata From The 5th Symphony	Widor	G. Schirmer, Kalmus
Trumpet Fanfare (Rondeau) (Theme from television series *Masterpiece Theatre*)	Mouret	Gentry, *Diane Bish Wedding Book*

Title	Composer	Publisher
Trumpet In Dialogue	Clerambault	Mercury, *Treasury Of Early Organ Music* ed. Biggs
Variations On A Theme From Hayden	Brahms	G. Schirmer
Wedding Processional And Air	Leupold	Augsburg

ORGAN COLLECTIONS

Title	Arranger	Publisher
Baroque Album, Vol. I & II.	arr. Wolff	Concordia
Baroque Music For Manuals, Vol. I & II.	arr. Wolff	Concordia
Bliss—Royal Fanfares and Interludes		Novello
Bloch—Four Wedding Marches		G. Schirmer
Book Of Wedding Pieces, A.		Oxford
Ceremonial Music For Organ, Book I & II.		Oxford
Classical Wedding Music, Vol. I & II.		Lorenz
Diane Bish Wedding Book	arr. Diane Bish	Gentry/Hinshaw
Gieschen—Organ Pieces For Wedding And General Use		Augsburg
Handel—Fireworks Music		Belwin
Handel—Suite From Water Music		J. Fisher
Handel—Water Music		Novello
Incidental Music For Weddings and Other Occasions, ed. Dearnley		Basil Ramsey
Modern Organ Music, Vol. I, II & III.		Oxford
Music For Weddings, ed. Rossine		Belwin
Second Book Of Wedding Pieces		Oxford
Three Trumpet Tunes	arr. David N. Johnson	Augsburg
Wedding Album For Manuals		Novello
Wedding Music, Book I, II, III, & IV.	arr. Johnson	Augsburg
Wedding Music, Vol. I & II.		Concordia

PIANO-ORGAN DUET BOOKS

Title	Arranger	Publisher
Easy Wedding Duets	arr. Lani Smith	Lorenz
Organ And Piano Duets For Church	arr. Setchell	R.D. Row
Schirmer's Album Of Organ And Piano Duets	arr. Stickles	G. Schirmer

ORGAN AND BRASS

Title	Arranger	Publisher
Bach/Biggs—My Spirit Be Joyful (O & Trpt)		Mercury
Bach/Biggs—Three Wedding Chorals		Associated

Title	Arranger	Publisher
Baroque Composers Of the Chapels Royal (O & 2 Trpt)	arr. Wolff	Concordia
Baroque Music For Weddings (O & 1 or 2 Trpt)	arr. Wolff	Concordia
Baroque Music For Organ (O & 1 or 2 Trpt)	arr. Wolff	Concordia
Bender—Wedding Sonata (O & Trpt, Trbn or Ob)		Hinshaw
Charpentier—Prelude To A Te Deum (O & Trpt)		Brass Press
Clarke/Kingsburg—Trumpet Voluntary in D (O & 3 Trpt)		Gray
Clark/Nelhybel—Trumpet Voluntary (O & 2 Trpt, 1 Trbn)		Hope
Gabrieli—Canzon Duodecimi Toni (O & BQ)		Augsburg
George—Wedding Music (O & Trpt)		Gray
Greene/Boyce—A Suite Of Trumpet Voluntaries (O & 2 "D" Trpt)		Brass Press
Handel/Wolff—Six Processionals (O & 1 or 2 Trpt)		Concordia
Johnson—Eight Fanfares For Organ And Brass (O & BQ)		Augsburg
Johnson—Festival Pieces For Brass (Processional O & Trpt)		Augsburg
Johnson—Tune For Trumpet (O & Trpt)		Augsburg
Marcello—Psalm XVIII (O & Trpt)		Gray
Mouret—Sinfonies De Fanfares (O & Trpt)		Gray
Music Of Jubilee (O & 1 or 2 Trpt)	arr. Wolff	Concordia
Powell—Antiphon For Two Trumpets and Organ		Concordia
Purcell—Sonata For Trumpet And Organ		Gray
Purcell—Suite In C Major (O & BQ)		Billaudot
Purcell—Three Celebrated Trumpet Tunes (O & Trpt)		GIA
Shaw—Grand Processional (O & B Sextet)		Sacred Music Press

Sinfonia A 2 Trombe (O & 2 "D" Trpt)		Brass Press
Skinnel—Wedding Processional (O & BQ)		Wimbledon
Stanley—Voluntary In Re Majeur (O & Trpt)		Billaudot
Strauss, R.—Festival Procession (O & 3 Trpt)		Lienau/Peters
Suite For Organ From The French Baroque (O & 1 or 2 Trpt)	arr. Wolff	Concordia
Telemann—Air De Trompette (O & Trpt)		Brass Press
Telemann—Airs For Trumpet And Organ		Gray
Telemann—Heroick Musick For Trumpet And Organ		SMP
Torelli—Sinfonia Con Tromba (O & Trpt)		King
Watson—Trumpet Tunes Revisited (O & Trpt)		Ludwig
Whitford—Four Trumpet And Organ Arrangements		J. Fisher
Zabel—Procession (O & BQ)		

ORGAN AND OTHER INSTRUMENTS

Alain, J.—Trois Movements (O & Flt)	LeDuc
Album Of 30 Classical Pieces, Vol. I & II (Flt & Piano)	International
Bach/Grace—Jesu Joy Of Man's Desiring (O & Vln)	Oxford
Bach/Grace—Sheep May Safely Graze (O & Strings)	Oxford
Classical Album (Oboe & Piano)	Boosey & Hawkes
Faure/Wilson—Pavae (Flt & Piano)	A. Broude
Flute Music Of The Baroque (Flt & Piano)	G. Schirmer
Satie—Three Gymnopedies (Clar, Flt or Oboe, Piano)	Elkan
Solos For The Oboe Player (Oboe, Piano)	G. Schirmer

VOCAL MUSIC FOR LITURGICAL WEDDINGS

Title	Composer	Publisher
Air (Cantata 202)	Bach	Assoc., Peters
Ave Maria	Gound	G. Schirmer, Carl Fisher
Be Thou With Them (Bist Du Bei Mir)	Bach	*Solos For The Church Year* by G. Schirmer
Behold, Thus Is The Man Blessed	Ferris	GIA
Beloved, Let Us Love One Another	Myers	Eastlane
Bless, O Lord, These Rings (solo or duet)	Roff	GIA
Bless Us. O God Of Loving	Wetzler	Augsberg
Blessed Are Those Who Fear The Lord	Powell	Concordia, *In Three Wedding Songs*
Blessed Are Those Who Fear The Lord (Psalm 128)	Sinzheimer	Concordia
Brother James' Air	Jacob	Oxford
Build Thee More Stately Mansions	Weaver	Galaxy
Call, The	Vaughn Williams	Boosey & Hawkes
Cantata 210 (O Holder Tag, Erwunschtezeit)	Bach	Associated
Canticle Of The Bride	Talbot	Cherry Lane
Come Down, O Love Divine	Vaughn Williams	Hymnals
Come My Beloved	Overby	Augsberg
Come, Lord Jesus, To This Place	Busarow	Concordia
Entreat Me Not To Leave Thee	Gore	Concordia
Entreat Me Not To Leave Thee	Gound	G. Schirmer
Entreat Me Not To Leave Thee	White	Concordia
Entreat Me Not To Leave Thee	Young	Galaxy
Eternal Life ("Prayer Of St. Francis")	Dungan	Presser
Evergreen (not the popular song from *A Star Is Born*)	Tanner	Warner Brothers
Father, All Creating	Butehude	Concordia, *Wedding Blessings*
Father, All Creating, O	Fetler	Concordia, *Wedding Blessings*
Flesh Of My Flesh	Patillo	Word
Gift Of Love (traditional)	Hopson	Hope
Gift To Be Simple, The	Parker	Hinshaw
God, A Woman and A Man	Green	Icthus

Title	Composer	Publisher
God Is My Shepherd	Dvorak	L.C. Fischer, *Dvorak Biblical Songs*
God My Shepherd	Bach/ Dickinson	Belwin
God Of Love My Shepherd Is	Thiman	Gray
God Of Love, O	Lovelace	Augsburg
God Of Love, O	Niccum	Bock, in *Whom God Hath Joined Together*
God Of Love, O	Wood	AMSI
Greatest Of These Is Love, The	Bitgood	Gray, Belwin, Augsburg
Greatest Of These Is Love, The	Dickau	Bock, in *Whom God Hath Joined Together*
Greatest Of These Is Love, The	Moe	Augsburg
Greatest Of These Is Love, The	Penhorwood	Hinshaw
Greatest Of These Is Love, The (All from 1st Corinthians 13)	Ware	Boston
Hallelujah (Alleluia)	Hummel	Belwin
Happy Are They Who Dwell In Your House	Pelz	Augsburg, *Three Solos For The High Voice*
Happy Are Those Who Fear The Lord (Psalm 128)	Schiavone	Concordia
Heart Worships, The	Holst	Galaxy
He Has Chosen You For Me	Terry	Word, in *Jubilation*
He Shall Give His Angels Charge Over Thee	Busarow	Concordia
How Amiable, O (2 part choral)	Vaughn Williams	Oxford
How Blest Are They	Proulx	Augsburg
How Do I Love Thee	Dello Joio	Carl Fischer
I Follow With Gladness	Bock	Paterson
I Love Thee	Beethoven	G. Schirmer
I Love Thee (Ich Liebe Dich)	Grieg	G. Schirmer
I Will Sing New Songs Of Gladness	Dvorak	G. Schirmer, C. Fischer in *Biblical Songs*
If With All Your Hearts	Mendelssohn	G. Schirmer
In His Care	Sateren	Augsburg

Title	Composer	Publisher
Entreat Me Not To Leave Thee	Oosting	Hope in *olk Songs For Weddings*
Jesu, Joy Of Loving Hearts	Brahms	Concordia in *Wedding Blessings*
Jesu, Joy Of Loving Hearts	Bach	Concordia in *Wedding Blessings*
Jesus, Shepherd Be Thou Near Me "Sheep May Safely Grace" melody	Bach	Concordia
Jesus Stand Beside Them	Lovelace	Concordia
King Of Love My Shepherd Is, The (choral)	Bairstow	Oxford
Lamps That Light This Wedding Day, The	Tallis/ Busarow	Concordia
Lord Bless You, The (duet)	Bach	Concordia
Lord Is My Shepherd, The	O'Conner/ Morris	Paterson
Lord, May Their Lives	Carroll	GIA
Lord, Who At Cana's Wedding Feast	Buxtehude	Concordia in *Wedding Blessings*
Lord, Who At Cana's Wedding Feast	Held	Augsburg in *Three Solos For Medium Voice*
Lord's Prayer, The	Malotte	G. Schirmer
Lord's Prayer, The	Peeters	Peters
Love, In Christ	Schultz	Concordia
Love Is Of God	Baumgartner	Concordia
Love Is The Sunlight "Morning Has Broken" tune	Busarow	Concordia
Love That Casts Out Fear	Bach	Concordia in *Wedding Blessings*
Marriage Prayer, A	Wetherill	Flammer "O Perfect Love" text
May God Smile On You (duet)	Bach	Peters
May The Grace Of Christ, Our Savior	Davies	Hymnal
May They In Thee Be One	MacNutt	BMI "O God Of Love" text
My Heart Ever Faithful	Bach	G. Schirmer
My Treasure	Brown	Cherry Lane
My Tribute	Crouch	Lexicon

Title	Composer	Publisher
Ninety First Psalm	MacDermid	Foster
Now With Thanksgiving	Busarow	Concordia
Nuptial Blessings	Proulx	Augsburg
O Lord Most Holy (Panis Angelicus)	Franck	G. Schirmer, others
O Master, Let Me Walk With Thee	Smith	Shawnee
On Eagles' Wings	Joncas	NALR
One In Heart And One In Mind	Bach/Roff	Abingdon
Only In The Beginning	Cull	Benson
Perfect Love, O (common hymn tune)	Barnby	Shawnee, C. Fischer
Perfect Love, O	Bock	Bock, in *Whom God Hath Joined Together*
Perfect Love, O	Burleigh	Presser
Perfect Love, O	Campbell-Watson	C. Fischer
Perfect Love, O	Harkor	G. Schirmer
Perfect Love, O	Fox	G. Schirmer C. Fischer
Perfect Love, O	Nystedt	Augsburg
Perfect Love, O	Sowerby	Gray, Belwin
Perfect Love, O	White	Hope in *Folk Songs For Weddings*
Perfect Love, O	Willan	Gray, Belwin
Perfect Love, O	Williams	Kjos
Prayer Of St. Francis	Temple	Found in *Songs Of Praise II*
Psalm 128	Dailey	Lillenas in *Bond Of Love*
Psalm 128	Wetzler	Augsberg
Simple Gifts (Old American Songs)	Copland	Boosey-Hawkes
Sacred Trust	Kreutz	GIA
Set Me As A Seal	Rochberg	Presser in *Four Songs Of Solomon* by Rochberg
Set Me As A Seal Upon Your Heart	Mitcheltree	Augsburg
Since Thou, O Fondest And Truest	Willan	Harris in *Song Album* by Willan

Song For A Christian Wedding	Girard	Word
Song Of Ruth	Eben	Word
Song Of Ruth	Hallquist	Hope in *Everything For The Wedding Soloist*
Song Of Ruth	Reagan	NALR in *Like A Seal On Your Heart*
Sweet, Sweet Spirit	Akers	Manna
Symbol, The	Niles	Mark Foster
Thanks Be To Thee	Handel	C. Fischer, others
That's The Way	Terry	Word
This Is The Day	Brown	Cherry Lane
This Love	Busarow	Concordia
Thou Art My Joy (Bist Du Bei Mir)	Bach	G. Schirmer
Thou Wilt Keep Him In Perfect Peace	Thiman	H.W. Gray
Thou Wilt Keep Him In Perfect Peace	Wienhorst	Concordia
Though I Speak With The Tongues	Brahms	Various editions, *Four Serious Songs*
Three Wedding Songs Abide With Them, Dear Savior O Perfect Love Lord, Who At Cana's Wedding	Cassler	Augsburg
Three Wedding Songs Our Heart Shall Rejoice In The Lord Blessed Are Those Who Fear The Lord May The Lord Watch Over This House	Powell	Concordia
To Grace A Marriage Feast	Ingalls	Eastlane in *Six Songs Of Early Americans For Church*
Together	Strader	Belwin
Two Candles	Salsbury	Word
Two Scriptural Songs We Wait In Hope For The Lord (with flute) The Greatest Of These Is Love	Wetzler	AMSI
Two Wedding Songs Lord, Bless The Souls Who Pledge Their Love O God Of Love	Butler	Sacred Music Press

Title	Composer	Publisher
Unity Candle Song, The	Sullivan & Hahn	GIA
Until	Collister	Wind-Chimes
Voice Of My Beloved	Helfman	Alex Broude
Voice That Breathed O'er Eden	Hullah/ Berenbroick	C. Fischer
Walk Hand In Hand	Cowell	Columbia
Walk In Love	Powell	Concordia
We Lift Our Hearts To Thee	Lovelace	G. Schirmer
Wedding Benediction, A	Lovelace	G. Schirmer
Wedding Blessing	Bunjes	Concordia, *Wedding Blessing,* ed. by Bunjes
Wedding Blessing	Grieb	C. Fischer
Wedding Blessing same text as Proulx "Nuptial Blessings"	Pelz	Augsburg
Wedding Cantata #202 (Weichet Nur, Betrubte Schatten)	Bach	Assoc., Peters
Wedding Hymn (Father In Heaven Abiding) tune from "Ptolemy"	Handel	BMI
Wedding Prayer, A (based on Bach theme)	Artman	Flammer
Wedding Prayer, A	Diggle	G. Schirmer
Wedding Prayer (Heavenly Father, Hear Us As We Pray)	Dunlap	G. Schirmer
Wedding Prayer, A	MacMillan	Paraclete
Wedding Prayer, A	Rice	Cherry Lane
Wedding Prayer, A	Williams	Gray
Wedding Prayer, A	Wilson	Lorenz
Wedding Processional and Air Based on finale of Cantata 202 (Wedding)	Bach / Leupold	Augsburg
Wedding Song (Psalm 128)	Bender	Concordia
Wedding Song	Carroll / Heckel	GIA
Wedding Song "Song Of Ruth" text	Gieseke	Concordia
Wedding Song "The Voice That Breathed O'er Eden"	MacMillan	Paraclete
Wedding Song "Song Of Ruth"	Peeters	Peters
Wedding Song "Set Me As A Seal	Pinkham	Peters
Wedding Song (folk tune "The Gift Of Love")	Routley	Hinshaw
Wedding Song "Song Of Ruth"	Schuetz	Chantry
Wedding Song	R. Verdi	GIA
When Adam Was Created	Bock	Gentry

When God Designed Creation	Busarow	Concordia
When Jesus To The Wedding Went	Glaser/ Busarow	Concordia
Westminster Abbey Hymn "Christ Is Made The Sure Foundation"	Purcell	Hymnal 1982
Where'er You Walk (from "Semele")	Handel	G. Schirmer
Wherever You Go	Norbet	NALR, *Glory And Praise #3. Gather To Remember, Wherever You Go*
Wither Thou Goest	Cassler	Augsburg
Wither Thou Goest	Dewey	Bock in *Whom God Hath Joined Together*
Wither Thou Goest	Hildach	Broude
Wither Thou Goest	Liljestrand	Hope in *Everything For The Wedding Soloist*
With Thou Goest	Singer	Hal Leonard
With This Ring	Matesky	Mercury
Within The Arc Of Grace	Edwards/ Busarow	Concordia

DUETS

And Now We Join	Halfvarson	Hope in *Everthing For The Wedding Soloist*
Beginning Today	Ducote	NALR in *Like A Seal On Your Heart*
Bless, O Lord, These Rings	Roff	GIA
Gift Of Love, The	Hopson	Hope in *Folk Songs For Weddings*
Greatest Of These Is Love	Bitgood	Gray
Lord Bless You, The	Bach	Concordia
Mary's Song	Joncas	NALR in *Like A Seal On Your Heart*

Title	Composer	Publisher
May God Smile On You	Bach	Peters
Love Divine, All Loves Excelling	Stainer	G. Schirmer
Only A Shadow	Landry	NALR in *Like A Seal On Your Heart*
Rainbow	Ducote	NALR in *Like A Seal On Your Heart*
There Is Only One Love	Danner	Triune in *Love Is The Melody*
Wedding Anthem (Psalm 128 text)	Oliver	Novello
Wedding Cantana (Vergnugte Pleissenstadt)	Bach	Associated
Wedding Prayer	Ault	NALR in *Like A Seal On Your Heart*
Wedding Prayer	Dunlap	G. Schirmer
Whither Thou Goest	Hildach	Broude

VOCAL MUSIC FOR NON-LITURGICAL WEDDING

Title	Composer	Publisher
Amazing Grace	Collins	Hal Leonard
And I Love You So	McLean	Columbia
Annie's Song	Denver	Cherry Lane
Beautiful	Lightfoot	Warner Bros.
Benedictus	Simon & Garfunkel	
Bridge Over Troubled Waters	Simon & Garfunkel	Hal Leonard
Candle On The Water	Kasha Hirschhorn	Cherry Lane
Can't Help Falling In Love	Peretti/Creatire/Weiss	Hal Leonard
Colour My World	Pankow	Columbia
Could I Have This Dance		Hal Leonard
Devoted To You	Bryant	Columbia
Endless Love		Hal Leonard
Evergreen	Streisand/Williams	Warner Bros.
Farewell Andromeda	Denver	Cherry Lane
First Time I Ever Saw Your Face	McColl	Columbia
Follow Me	Denver	Cherry Lane
For All We Know	Wilson/James/Karlin	Columbia
For Baby (For Bobby)	Denver	Cherry Lane
Forever Young	Dylan	Warner Bros.
The Hands Of Time (Brian's Song)	Legrand	Warner Bros.
Hawaiian Wedding Song		Hal Leonard
Hopelessly Devoted To You	Farrar	Hal Leonard
I Can't Help Falling In Love		Columbia

Song	Composer	Publisher
I Don't Know How To Love Him	Rice/Webber	Hal Leonard
I Honestly Love You	Allen/Barry	Columbia
I Just Want To Be Your Everything	Gibb	Hal Leonard
I Only Want To Be With You		Hal Leonard
I Won't Last A Day Without You	Williams	Columbia
If	Gates	Warner Bros.
If Ever I Would Leave You		Hal Leonard
If I Were A Carpenter	P. P. Mary	Columbia
If We Only Have Love	Brel	Hal Leonard
I'll Never Be Alone	McJuen	
I'll Never Find Another You (The Promised Land)	The Seekers	
In My Life	Lennon/McCartney	Cherry Lane
Just The Way You Are	Joel	Columbia
Let It Be	Lennon/McCartney	Cherry Lane
Let It Be Me	Becaud	Hal Leonard
Let's Get Together	Powers	
Longer	Fogelberg	Columbia
Look To The Rainbow	Lane	Hal Leonard
Lord Of The Dance	Carter	
Love	Lennon	Cherry Lane
Love Is A Many Splendored Thing	Webster/Fain	Columbia
Love Me Tender	Presley/Matson	Hal Leonard
Love Song	Murray	Warner Bros.
Love Song, A	Loggins	
Love Story	Lai	Columbia
More	Ortolani/Oliviero	Hal Leonard
Morning Has Broken	Stevens	Warner Bros.
My Cup Runneth Over	Jones	Hal Leonard
My Sweet Lady	Denver	Cherry Lane
My Treasure	Brown	Sparrow Birdwing
Nadia's Theme	DeVorzon & Botkin	Warner Bros
Our Love	Carpenters	
People	Streisand	Hal Leonard
People Alone (The Competition)		Columbia
Perhaps Love	Denver	Cherry Lane
Poems, Prayers, and Promises	Denver	Cherry Lane
The Rose	McBroom	Warner Bros.
So Many Ways	King	
Sometimes	Mancini	Columbia
Song Is Love, The	P. P. Mary	Warner Bros.
Sound Of Music	Rogers and Hammerstein	Hal Leonard

Speak, Softly Love	Rota	
Starting Here, Starting Now	Maltby	Hal Leonard
Sunrise, Sunset	Harnick & Bock	Hal Leonard
Sunshine On My Shoulders	Denver	Cherry Lane
That's The Way	Terry	Sparrow Birdwing
This Is The Day	Brown	
Through The Eyes Of Love	Sager/Hamlisch	Columbia
Till There Was You	Wilson	Hal Leonard
Time For Us, A	Rota/Kusik/Snyder	Columbia
Time In A Bottle	Croce	Warner Bros.
To Love	Cason/Gibb	
Today	Sparks	Columbia
Together Forever	Jones	
Top Of The World	Carpenters	Columbia
True Love	Porter	Hal Leonard
Truly	Richie	Cherry Lane
Try To Remember		Hal Leonard
Turn, Turn, Turn	Birds	Hal Leonard
Twelfth Of Never	Mathis	Hal Leonard
Up Where We Belong		Columbia
Wedding Song	Collins	
Wedding Song (There Is Love)	Stookey	Warner Bros.
You've Only Just Begun	Williams/Nichols	Columbia
What A Difference You've Made In My Life	Jordan	Hal Leonard
What Are You Doing The Rest O Your Life	Lagrand	
Whenever I Call You Friend	Loggins	Warner Bros.
With You I'm Born Again	Conners/Shire	Columbia
Wonder Of You, The	Knight	Hal Leonard
Would You Walk With Me?	Colter	
You And I	Wonder	Columbia
You Are The Sunshine Of My Life	Wonder	Columbia
You Light Up My Life	Brooks	Columbia
You Needed Me	Goodrum, Murray	Hal Leonard

SELECTING MUSICIANS FOR YOUR WEDDING

The following outline gives you some basic and general ideas to consider in choosing the musicians for your wedding, as well as the various instruments that might included in the ceremony. The choice of repertoire that would be deemed appropriate for a wedding is vast; therefore keep in mind that this list is not a specific list, but a general one. Also notice that there are pieces that are written specifically for organ and instruments. In a large number of cases the piano part can be modified for organ, should a piano not be available. Many churches require that their own musicians be responsible for all weddings performed there.

I. Your Musicians/Music Ministers
  A. How many?
    1. During what parts of the service and reception are they going to play?
    2. Most musicians should receive some type of payment. How much can you afford and how much are their fees?
      a. This should be discussed early.
      b. "Union" musicians will require union scale pay.
    3. What level of performance capability are you seeking?
      a. A friend's performance, possibly non-professional.
      b. Professional job (are you going to record the ceremony?)
      c. How long would you like the musicians' perfomance to be?
        1. Prelude before the service?
        2. During the service?
        3. After the service?
        4. At the reception?
      d. Some amateurs may not have the "stamina" to last through a long session.
  B. Where do you find your musicians?
    1. Friends, family members
      a. If you're using more than one performer, are their playing levels compatible?
      b. Can they handle a wedding performance?
        1. Nervousness?
        2. Music at their ability level to avoid unnecessary pressure?
      c. Do they have their instrument in playable condition?
    2. Performers
      a. Local college or school.
      b. Small performance ensembles who regularly meet and are willing to take on a wedding.
    3. Professionals
      a. Referral services.

b. Musicians' union.
c. Established performance groups.

II. The Music
A. Who chooses the music?
1. If you choose the music—
a. Talk it over with your musicians first, maintaining constant communication with the church personnel. **very important!**
1. How difficult should the arrangement be?
2. The harder the music, the more practice and rehearsal required.
3. Do they have any suggestions for suitable material?
b. Popular music.
1. Very few arrangements are available with instrumental parts.
2. Check with your instrumentalist regarding range and transposing.
3. **Be sure to check with your church on requirements,** as many will not allow the use of popular music because of the sacredness of the rite.
2. If the musicians choose the music.
a. Give them exact times during the service you would like them to play.
b. Talk over particular titles and/or composers, or eras (Baroque, Romantic) of music you would like to have.
B. Who pays for the music?
1. If you're dealing with professional musicians, they may have their own library to draw from.
2. If you have friends doing the service—
a. Do they have music on hand that is suitable?
b. Bride and groom are responsible for music expense. How much do you wish to spend?

III. Rehearsals
A. When using instruments plus organ or piano accompaniment.
1. Soloist may want to rehearse with organist/pianist previous to church rehearsal. Arrangements should be made.

2. It is advisable to have a rehearsal at the church or hall if it can be scheduled so the other musicians can practice with the organ/piano they will be using.

B. When using multiple instrument groups.
   1. If professional musicians or a group who rehearse together on a regular basis are used, there should be no problem with extra rehearsals. If you hire professionals, a rehearsal at the church **may** cost extra.
   2. If friends or family members are playing.
      a. Extra rehearsals are advised, just to get the feel of playing together.
      b. Rehearsal in the church or reception area will allow the musicians time to make adjustments for acoustics.
   3. Have a clear order of performance and signals.
      a. Make sure the musicians know the order in which the pieces are scheduled.
      b. Have your musicians' cue worked out beforehand.
         1. When to start (prelude or postlude.)
         2. When to finish (prelude or postlude.)
         3. Actual cue words or gestures for performance during the ceremony.
   4. Double check equipment needs.
      a. Do the musicians need—
         1. Special chairs?
         2. Stands?
      b. Do you need to make any special provisions for the "sound" system?
         1. Extra microphones (classical guitars, flute)
         2. Extra speakers (electric guitars, electric pianos, etc.)

Popular Instrumental Combinations for Weddings

I. Woodwinds
   A. Trio
      1. Flute, oboe, clarinet
      2. Oboe, clarinet, bassoon
   B. Quintet
      1. Flute, oboe, clarinet, horn, bassoon
      2. Oboe, clarinet, horn, bassoon, piano

II. Brass
- A. Quartet
  1. Two trumpets, horn, trombone
  2. Two trumpets, two trombones
- B. Quintet—two trumpets, horn, trombone, tuba

III. Strings
- A. Trio—violin, cello, piano
- B. Quartet—two violins, viola, cello

IV. Woodwind and string quartets
- A. Flute, violin, viola, cello
- B. Oboe, violin, viola, cello

V. Trio sonatas
- A. Two flutes, bassoon (cello) basso continuo (piano, harpsicord or organ)
- B. Flute, oboe, bassoon (cello) and basso continuo
- C. Two violins, bassoon (cello) and basso continuo
- D. Flute, violin, bassoon (cello) and basso continuo
- E. Violin, oboe, bassoon (cello) and basso continuo

NOTES

____

____

____

____

____

____

____

____

CHECKLIST FOR CEREMONY MUSIC

* Note—All music requirements of the local church are to be taken into consideration when planning your music selections.

PRELUDE
Time/Cue: ____________ Selection: ____________
Selection: ____________ Selection: ____________
Selection: ____________ Selection: ____________

FIRST SOLO
Time/Cue: ____________ Selection: ____________

PROCESSIONAL
Time/Cue: ____________ Selection: ____________

BRIDE'S ENTRANCE
Time/Cue: ____________ Selection: ____________

SECOND SOLO
Time/Cue: ____________ Selection: ____________

RECESSIONAL
Time/Cue: ____________ Selection: ____________

POSTLUDE
Time/Cue: ____________ Selection: ____________

MUSICIANS
____________ Cost: ____________
____________ Cost: ____________
____________ Cost: ____________
____________ Cost: ____________

SOLOISTS
____________ Cost: ____________
____________ Cost: ____________
Total Cost: ____________

WEDDING PROGRAMS

If you are going to have printed wedding programs, generally the following information is included:

— Program Title
— Order of Service
— Acknowledgement of Participants
— Messages and Notations

PROGRAM TITLE

This sections is generally positioned at the top of the inside left-hand page for programs with full cover designs and usually includes the following:

DESCRIPTIVE PHRASE
BRIDE'S NAME
GROOM'S NAME
Day and Date
Time
Ceremony Location
City and State

Some suggestions for the descriptive phrase are:

THE WEDDING CEREMONY
of

THE SACRAMENT OF
HOLY MATRIMONY
UNITING

WELCOME TO
THE MARRIAGE SERVICE

THE CELEBRATION AND BLESSING
OF THE MARRIAGE UNITING

THE MARRIAGE CELEBRATION
of

THE WORSHIP SERVICE
UNITING IN MARRIAGE

THE WEDDING MASS
UNITING

THE WEDDING SERVICE
UNITING

ORDER OF SERVICE

The Order of Service outlines the individual service segments—Prelude, Processional, Solo, Invocation, Scripture Reading, Marriage Ceremony, Lighting of Unity Candle, Benediction, Recessional, etc. Depending on faith, the customs and liturgical terminology will vary. It is best to consult with your clergy regarding the service.

Other items to include are music titles with composers and/or performers, book and poem titles with authors and/or readers, scripture passages with readers, hymn titles with hymnal page numbers, words for short congregational prayers, and any special notations. Generally, there is not enough room to include entire songs or readings. If these items are not available in church hymnals or prayer books, they could be printed on the back side of the program. Permission to reprint copyrighted material must be gotten from the respective publisher.

PARTICIPANTS

Participants can be grouped and sequenced using titled headers to separate the groupings, or everyone can be listed in a logical sequence under the single heading "Wedding Participants." Be consistent with respect to naming individuals. Names should be preceded with titles such as Mrs., Ms., or Miss. Given names should be used, instead of nicknames.

MESSAGE AND NOTATION SECTION

This section can be positioned at the bottom of the right-hand page on the program's backside if blank. Short personal messages or expressions of thanks to the guests from the bride and groom are very appropriate and make for a lasting keepsake. As an alternative to the personal message, a special prayer, poem or short quotation might nicely express your feelings. Notations regarding the reception, picture-taking restriction, viewing of gifts, new home address or other information necessary for guests should be at the bottom of the page.

Following are some samples of personal messages or expressions of thanks you may want to have printed on your wedding programs, or spoken during the ceremony.

"Thank you for sharing this happy day with us."

"Thank you for sharing this service with us. You have added to our joy by being with us on our wedding day."

"We are honored you can share these sacred and joyous moments with us today. May God bless each one of you."

"Special thanks to everyone for sharing in this joy of ours today."

"Thank you for sharing this service with us on our wedding day."

"Thank you for sharing these precious moments with us and for witnessing our vows to each other. You are invited to the home of the groom at ________________, where the gifts may be seen following the reception."

"We would like to express our gratitude to our parents for their love and guidance. We also would like to thank our relatives and friends for coming today to share our joy. We ask God's blessing and your prayers upon our marriage."

"Especially for our parents—Thank you for bringing us to this day. We have learned love from you and hope in our marriage to always return it to you."

"To our parents, who have been so patient and understanding and have given us so much love and encouragement, thank you. On this very special day in our lives, we want you to know WE LOVE YOU VERY MUCH!"

"We would also like to express our gratitude to the many others who have freely given of their ideas, support and labor to make this day possible."

"Thank you for sharing this special day with us. That so many of our friends and family, especially those who came from such great distances, could be here to help us celebrate our marriage means a great deal to us. We pray that God will grant you a safe journey to your homes when the festivities have ended. May He always bless and enrich your lives with joy and love as much as you have enriched ours with your friendship and generosity."

"It means a great deal to us to have each of you here today. Thank you for witnessing our expression of love for each other through the vows that begin our new life together. We feel that our love stems from our capacity to love deeply, enjoy simply, and to think freely. Our special wish is that each of you will continue to be a part of our lives. Without friends, family and parents, we have very little."

"As our hearts are joined and we begin our new life together, we pause to look at everyone here on our special day. We find it difficult to put into words our feelings to those who share our love and happiness. Words seldom go quite deep enough when thanks should be expressed. We would like at this time to thank those who wish us well. We would especially like to thank our parents and our brothers and sisters who not only wish us well, but who are always there when we need them. May God bless you always.

"To our families and friends—We are honored that you are here to help us celebrate this very important day in our lives. On this day, we shall vow our love and commitment to one another before God and you. It is our prayer that God be glorified in this service and each of you receive His blessing."

"WELCOME TO OUR WEDDING CEREMONY—We, the bride and groom, are honored to have you as our guests today. We want you to share these happy and sacred moments with us. May the blessing of the Lord be on all of us as we worship together. It is our desire that Christ shall be honored, not only in this ceremony. but in the years to come. We want him to be the head of our home and the Lord of our lives."

"We would like to express our sincerest thanks to all of you for helping us make this day a joyous celebration—especially our parents who gave us life; our families who shared our life; our relatives and friends who helped us grow up to this special day."

"TO OUR WEDDING GUESTS—Your presence here adds greatly to our joy and happiness on this day which marks the beginning of our lives together. We stand before you now, declaring before God and this congregation, our love for each other and our intent to be joined in marriage; to share with each other without reservation our lives, fortunes and future. We hope that you will continue to wish us well in our new life as you have done in the past, and will pray for our continued happiness and success."

RECEIVING LINE

Once the officiator has concluded the ceremony with the pronouncement of marriage, the recessional follows. (This is usually the processional in reverse.) The maid of honor gives the bride her bouquet and adjusts her train; the bride takes her grooms right arm and they exit first. The flower girl and ring bearer follow, then the maid of honor takes the best man's right arm and they exit. The bridesmaids and ushers then follow in pairs, a symbol of the marital union that has just been formed.

The ushers now return to escort mothers, grandmothers, and other older female relatives of the bride and groom, with bride's parents together first. Guests do the same by alternating left and right, row-by-row.

The receiving line already is being formed in the vestibule of the church if the clergy so permits. The receiving line follows the order of exit.

Now family and friends may file through the line offering their best wishes and congratulations.

NOTES

____

____

____

____

____

____

____

____

____

____

As a Flower
unfolds in the Sun...
So opens the Heart
to the tender warmth
of Love

Chapter 14

Flowers

FLOWERS

Flowers will enhance your wedding style, as well as add beauty and elegance at the ceremony and reception. It is suggested that you choose a reputable florist well in advance of the wedding date, as the most experienced ones tend to be reserved far in advance. The florist will be able to assist you in selecting the appropriate flowers to match your color scheme, advising you as to which ones are in season, etc.

Traditionally, the bride's family pays for floral decoration for the ceremony and reception, as well as the bridesmaids' bouquets. The groom provides the bride's bouquet and going-away corsage, corsages for mothers and grandmothers, and boutonnieres for himself, fathers, and all men in the wedding party.

FLOWERS FOR THE CEREMONY

The purpose of flowers at a church ceremony is to help enhance the worship space. These may range from vases of flowers to more elaborate arrangements with sprays of flowers lining the aisle. **Be sure to check with your clergyperson as to what the church allows.**

If you are being married at home or in a hotel or club, it is best to select an attractive spot such as a fireplace or large window and decide what floral arrangements will best enhance it. Again, your professional florist will be able to help you make your decision. Be aware of the fact that some churches do not allow silk or artificial flowers because they are contradictory to the symbol and tradition of freshness, purity, life, wholeness, etc. On the other hand, some may not allow potted flowers/plants inside the church. Also, the chancel area of the Protestant church is viewed much differently than the sanctuary of the Catholic church. In fact, most Catholic churches do not even allow any flowers **on** the altar.

FLOWERS FOR THE ATTENDANTS

The bridal bouquet is the most beautiful of all, but the gown you will be wearing will determine the type of bouquet you choose. The gown is still the main focus. Keep in mind that the bride's bouquet and her attendants' bouquets should be coordinated in theme and color. You may also choose to carry a white prayer book or small Bible. If the bride is wearing a street-length dress, she may choose to wear a corsage instead of carrying a bouquet.

If you show your florist swatches of your bridesmaids' dresses and sketches of the dress style, he/she will be able to suggest suitable bouquets and head pieces.

The bouquet for the maid (or matron) of honor may be slightly different from the bridesmaids' bouquets.

The flowers carried by a flower girl should be demure, as befits her age and size. A small basket or nosegay is best. Carrying a basket is easy and natural and gives her something to concentrate on as she walks down the aisle.

Corsages for mothers and grandmothers should be chosen with the color of their dresses in mind. They should be kept simple—a cymbidium orchid has been a favorite for many.

Boutonnieres for the men in the wedding party are simply a symbol of participation in the wedding, so they should be small and simple. Carnations are frequently used. but other possibilities include one white (or matching color) sweetheart rose, or a sprig of stephanotis. The groom's boutonniere is generally a flower of the same type as those in the bride's bouquet, and should be different from those of the other men in the wedding party.

Reception Flowers

Reception flowers should be coordinated with the wedding theme in both color and design. The buffet table is the center of attention and therefore the centerpiece should be elaborate. You will also need centerpieces for the table where the guests will be seated. You may also wish to use fresh flowers, or silk flowers, on your wedding cake. This can be done easily by your caterer or baker. The base of the cake can be garlanded with greens or surrounded by the wedding bouquets during the reception and for pictures.

Notes

____

____

____

____

____

FLOWER GUIDE

The flowers as listed will probably be available the year round, but it is wise to check with the florist before making a decision.

- African Daisies
- Baby's Breath
- Bachelor Buttons
- Cornflowers
- Carnations
- Delphiniums
- Gardenias
- Gladioli
- Easter Lilies
- Lilies-of-the-Valley
- Orchids
- Roses
- Snapdragons
- Stephanotis
- Ivy

The following flowers are usually available for autumn weddings:

- Asters
- Chrysanthemums
- Dahlias
- Shasta Daisies
- Autumn leaves & foliage
- Tuberoses
- Zinnias
- Spider Mums
- Shaggy-petaled Fujis

The following flowers are usually available for winter weddings:

- Acacia
- Calla Lilies
- Camellias
- Forget-Me-Nots
- Iris
- Lilacs
- Poinsettias (white or red)
- Madonna Lilies
- Sweet Peas
- Tulips
- Winter greens or holly

The following flowers are usually available for springtime weddings:

- Apple Blossoms
- Calla Lilies
- Daffodils
- Easter Lilies
- Dogwood
- Geraniums
- Forsythia Branches
- Forget-Me-Nots
- Iris
- Lilacs
- Jonquils
- Larkspur
- Narcissus
- Peonies
- Sweet Peas
- Tulips
- Violets

The following flowers are usually available for summertime weddings:

- Asters
- Calla Lilies
- Daisies
- Forget-Me-Nots
- Iris
- Larkspur
- Peonies
- Shasta Daisies
- Snowballs
- Stock
- Sweet Peas
- Tuberoses
- Zinnias
- Queen Anne's Lace

Again, this is just a guideline—check with your local florist as to what is available.

Florist Checklist

FLORIST'S NAME:____________ PHONE #:__________

ADDRESS: ____________________

Wedding Party Flowers

*BRIDE'S BOUQUET STYLE: ____ BOUQUET COLOR: __

KINDS OF FLOWERS: __________ RIBBON COLOR:____

______________________________ COST:____________

*BRIDEMAIDS' STYLE: _________ BOUQUET COLOR__

KINDS OF FLOWERS: __________ RIBBON COLOR:____

______________________________ COST:

______________________________ QUANTITY: ________

*MAID OF HONOR'S STYLE:____ BOUQUET COLOR: __

KINDS OF FLOWERS: __________ RIBBON COLOR:____

______________________________ COST:____________

*CORSAGES – BRIDE'S MOTHER, GROOM'S MOTHER, GRANDMOTHERS, ETC.

CORSAGE COLOR:____________ RIBBON COLOR:____

KINDS OF FLOWERS: __________ COST:____________

______________________________ QUANTITY: ________

*BOUTONNIERES – GROOM'S: __ COLOR:____________

KIND OF FLOWER: ____________ COST:____________

*BOUTONNIERES - BEST MAN, GROOMSMEN, USHERS, FATHERS:

KIND OF FLOWERS:____________ COST:____________

QUANTITY: ____________________ COST:____________

Our love
brings new meaning to life

CEREMONY FLOWERS

*ALTAR ARRANGEMENTS:______ COLOR:____________

KINDS OF FLOWERS: __________ QUANTITY: ________

______________________________ COST:_____________

*PEW MARKERS: ______________ COLOR:____________

KINDS OF FLOWERS: __________ QUANTITY: ________

______________________________ COST:_____________

* OTHER

AISLE RUNNER: _______________ KNEE CUSHION:____

* DELIVERY INFORMATION

WHICH FLOWERS:__________________________________

DATE:________________________ TIME:______________

ADDRESS: ____

NOTES

____

____

____

____

____

____

____

RECEPTION FLOWERS

HEAD TABLE ARRANGEMENTS: COLOR:___________
KINDS OF FLOWERS: __________ QUANTITY: _______
______________________________ COST:____________
GUEST TABLE
ARRANGEMENTS:______________ COLOR:___________
KINDS OF FLOWERS: __________ QUANTITY: _______
______________________________ COST:____________
BUFFET TABLE
ARRANGEMENTS:______________ COLOR:___________
KINDS OF FLOWERS: __________ QUANTITY: _______
______________________________ COST:____________
RECEIVING LINE:______________ COLOR:___________
KINDS OF FLOWERS: __________ QUANTITY: _______
______________________________ COST:____________
WEDDING CAKE TABLE:_______ COLOR:___________
KINDS OF FLOWERS: __________ QUANTITY: _______
______________________________ COST:____________
OTHER ARRANGEMENTS: _____ COLOR:___________
KINDS OF FLOWERS: __________ QUANTITY: _______
______________________________ COST:____________

DELIVERY INFORMATION

WHICH FLOWERS:___________________________________
DATE:________________________ TIME:_____________
ADDRESS: ____

TOTAL COST OF ALL FLOWERS: ____________

NOTES

Love
is like the
song of morning
Sunlight on dew—
Bright, beautiful and
always new

Chapter 15

Photography/Videography

PHOTOGRAPHY

You should choose a reputable, professional photographer specializing in wedding pictures. Begin your search for a photographer far in advance of the wedding date (up to a year or more) as many of the best photographers are booked up to a year or two ahead of time. Ask to see entire albums of recent weddings they have done. Find out what exactly is included in their "package price"—number of shots, time photographer will work, if album is included, etc.

Meet with the person who will actually be taking the photos. Explain the formals and informals that you want taken. Discuss any church restrictions, and ask your photographer to be as inconspicuous as possible. Also, appoint a friend or cousin to help the photographer round up special people, etc., so that your day isn't spent worrying about getting everyone together. Many couples today are having their **posed** church pictures taken before the service so as not to hold up the families/friends afterward.

Following is a helpful guide to be sure all those happy memories are captured on film. Be sure to ask about the many other special effects photos that can be creatively done today.

BEFORE THE CEREMONY

___ Bride in dress.
___ Bride putting on veil.
___ Bride with mother.
___ Bride with father.
___ Bride with both parents.
___ Bride with honor attendants.
___ Bride with bridesmaids.
___ Bride with grandparents/godparents/special friends.
___ Bride with brothes and sisters.
___ Bride touching up makeup/hair.
___ Everyone getting flowers.
___ Bride leaving house.
___ Bride and father getting into car.
___ Groom alone.
___ Groom with best man.
___ Groomsmen getting boutonnieres.
___ Other ______________________________
___ ______________________________

AT THE CEREMONY

___ Guests outside the church.
___ Bride and father getting out of car.
___ Bride and father going into church.
___ Ushers escorting guests.
___ Groom's parents being seated (or in procession).
___ Bride's mother being seated (or in procession).
___ Soloist and/or organist.
___ Groom and groomsmen at altar (or in procession).
___ Giving-away ceremony
___ Altar or canopy during ceremony.
___ Each attendant as procession begins.
___ Bride and father waiting for procession to begin.
___ Procession of groom with his parents/bride with her parents. During the Mass or service, the photographer should be most discreet and not distract from the central action taking place.
___ Bridal party at the altar.
___ Bride and groom exchanging vows.
___ Ring ceremony.
___ Groom meeting bride.
___ The kiss.
___ Bride and groom coming up aisle.
___ Bride and groom on church steps.
___ Bride alone in the church.
___ Bride and groom amongst the guests, wedding party.
___ Bride and groom getting into car.
___ Bride and groom in back seat of car.
___ Other ____
___ ____
___ ____

NOTES

____
____
____
____

Posed Shots Before the Reception

___ Bridesmaids looking at bride's ring.
___ Bride's and groom's hands.
___ Bride and groom together.
___ Bride with parents.
___ Groom with parents.
___ Bride and groom with honor attendants.
___ Bride and groom with children.
___ Bride with her attendants.
___ Groom with his attendants.
___ Bride, groom, all the wedding party.
___ Bride, groom, all the parents.
___ Other ______________________________
___ ______________________________
___ ______________________________

Notes

At the Reception

___ Bride and groom arriving.
___ Bride and groom getting out of car.
___ Bride and groom going into reception.
___ The receiving line (posed).
___ The receiving line (candid).
___ Bride and groom in receiving line.
___ Bride's mother in receiving line.
___ Groom's parents in receiving line.
___ Buffet table.
___ Friends serving punch.
___ Bride and groom at bridal table.
___ Parents' table.
___ Entire wedding party at table.
___ Bride and groom dancing.
___ Bride and her father dancing.
___ Groom and his mother dancing.
___ The musicians.
___ Bride and groom talking to guests.
___ Guest book table.
___ The cake table.
___ Bride and groom cutting the cake.
___ Bride and groom feeding each other cake.
___ Bride and groom toasting.
___ Throwing and catching the bouquet.
___ Groom taking off bride's garter.
___ Throwing and catching the garter.
___ Wedding party decorating car.
___ Bride changing into going-away clothes.
___ Groom changing into going-away clothes.
___ Bride and groom saying goodbye to parents.
___ Bride and groom ready to leave.
___ Guests throwing rice.
___ Guests waving goodbye.
___ Rear of car when leaving.
___ Other ____
___ ____
___ ____
___ ____

WEDDING PHOTOGRAPHY CHECKLIST

Photographer's Name:______________ Phone #: __________

Address: ____

COST:

Guaranteed rate?______ Deposit: _____ Amount?________

When is deposit due? ______ When is balance due? __________

How does the photographer bill me?_________________________

How long is the photographerat the ceremony?_ Reception?____

Cancellation terms: _____________________________________

____

FORMAL ENGAGEMENT PICTURES

Size: ________ Price: ________ Size: ________ Price: ________

Size: ________ Price: ________ Size: ________ Price: ________

FORMAL WEDDING PICTURES

Price: _____

CANDID PRE-CEREMONY PICTUERS

Size: ________ Price: ________ Size: ________ Price: ________

Size: ________ Price: ________ Size: ________ Price: ________

CANDID CEREMONY PICTURES

Size: ________ Price: ________ Size: ________ Price: ________

Size: ________ Price: ________ Size: ________ Price: ________

CANDID RECEPTION PICTURES

Size: ________ Price: ________ Size: ________ Price: ________

Size: ________ Price: ________ Size: ________ Price: ________

PROOFS

How many proofs will be made?_____________________________

What size will proofs be?__________________________________

Will I be able to purchase the proofs not used?______________

Cost: $ ____

Will an album be provided? ______________________________

Family albums? ______________________________

What date will the finished pictures be ready?________________

Shortly after the wedding date, your photographer will notify you that your proofs are developed. You and your new husband can then select the shots you will want enlarged for your album. Keep in mind that your wedding photographs are an investment for your memory and for your new future. They also make nice gifts for friends and relatives who share in your joy and love!

NOTES

____

____

____

____

____

____

____

____

____

____

____

____

____

____

____

____

____

____

Photographers/Videotape Services

Videotaping, the newest fashion in wedding memories, promises to become as much of a tradition as still photographs. The equipment is lightweight and portable, allowing as much flexibility and scope as you want and are willing to finance. Tape players have fast forward and rewind features for pinpointing your favorite scenes any time you're feeling nostalgic.

How to Order

Select your wedding and reception sites before interviewing companies to be aware of restrictions on videotaping activities or lighting and power problems. Some religious denominations prohibit videotaping; others allow it but restrict auxiliary lighting to maintain a dignified atmosphere. Low lighting may not rule out taping but the quality will be grainier.

Videotaping wedding services are relatively new. They require careful comparisons. Look for broad experience in commercial and industrial work to find the seasoned professionals. Keep a record on the worksheet of the information you gather.

Preview samples of the company's past work. Ask for a description of the proposed scenario and how many cameras are necessary to do it well. Productions range from a single camera shooting from one angle to several roving ones. The best tapes tell a story rather than show unrelated clips. Although you want to rely on the professional's experience, a good producer wants to know your expectations and preferences.

Encourage the video producer and still photographer to coordinate their plans beforehand for maximum, effective use of each medium.

Two types of productions are available. One, the least expensive, uses one camera in more stationary positions. Shots are taken as the action unfolds and there's no post-production work. That means no editing, no customizing and no music although you have the option of adding these later at additional costs. The church shots, for example, are taken with one stationary camera. If a bridal party member gets in the line of sight or you and the groom have to turn your backs to the camera, that's what the completed tape will show.

More expensive productions use at least two roving cameras and remake the tape by editing. The cost increases with the complexity. An elaborate production may cost five or six times that of a simple, unedited tape.

VIDEOTAPE TECHNIQUES

Directors have a variety of techniques at their command. Color tape and dual audio (microphones) are available. Your wedding music can be taped during the festivities and dubbed in later. Some tapes start with titles and a montage of 2-3-second clips, and it's possible to include interviews with friends and relatives.

WHAT IT COSTS

Total cost will depend on equipment, how long the crew works, what graphics are added, and the tape length, sound dubbing, photographic special effects and editing which is often the biggest cost. Equipment ranges from "home movie" video cameras to high resolution, broadcast quality cameras. Generally, companies charge an hourly rate, though some set a flat fee. Decide what your wedding budget will allow and choose within those limits.

WHY VIIDEO

Many churches are promoting the use of video today because it offers the most realistic memory of your wedding. You are most nervous during the ceremony. So nervous that you may not even remember the details. A video allows you to sit with family and friends afterward to view the wedding, sharing the many wonderful highlights together.

The reception, on the other hand, is full of fun and excitement. So many people to greet, so many things going on — even some family you may not have seen in years.. What a perfect way to remember the faces, the fun, the moments like... your wedding waltz, your favorite song, a special song, a stolen kiss... My recommendation on videotaping the reception is to pay by the hour and save every inch of film, unedited. You will be happy you did.

The videotaping makes a great gift to friends far away. It can also make an anniversary very special. The memory of your wedding can live on and on.

NOTES

In the sweetness of love
let there be laughter
and in all our tomorrows
the freshness of today

Chapter 16

Transportation

WEDDING DAY TRANSPORTATION

A very important part of planning your wedding day is arranging the transportation. After all, you want to make sure that you, the wedding party, your parents, and the guests all get to the church and reception on time!

The bride is traditionally responsible for making transportation arrangements to the church for herself, her parents, the bridesmaids, and also the groom's parents. The classic way to travel on your wedding day is by a nice, shiny limousine. Check around for rates and availability. Otherwise, ask your friends or relatives if their cars would be available to use. Offer to pay for gas and a car wash, and thank them with a small gift.

On the wedding day, have all the cars arrive at your house in time to reach the church at least 15 minutes before the ceremony. If you will be dressing at the church, allow extra time. Plan all your at-home candids well in advance of your leaving for church. In the first car should be your mother with your honor attendant, and perhaps another bridesmaid or two; the second car has the rest of your bridesmaids; the third car is for you and your father. Of course, you will have a chauffeur driving these cars. A separate car can pick up the groom's parents. You're on your way! The groom and his best man should take care of their own transportation to the church. They should get there at least 15 minutes to a half hour before the ceremony so that the best man has enough time to give the clergyperson the fee, and also to help the groom straighten his tie and calm any pre-wedding jitters!

If you have many out-of-town guests coming to your wedding, be sure they know how to get to the church and to the reception hall. If you live in a large city, you may want to have maps made up giving directions. These can be included with the invitation, or may be handed out after the ceremony. Reserve parking for the wedding party cars.

When leaving the church, you and your new husband ride in one car—the one that brought you, and your father to the church. Your parents and the groom's parents travel to the reception in their own cars, bridesmaids and ushers in the remaining cars. Chances are that your attendants will slip away during the reception to decorate your getaway car. Or, some friends may do this during the ceremony. Have the groom drop some hints as to how he would like the cars decorated. Decorations should be safe and should not obstruct the driver's vision. If you plan to honk horns as you drive through the city, be considerate of neighborhood residents, hospital zones, etc. Drive safely!

TRANSPORTATION

You'll feel so special on your wedding day, and look so grand, you deserve to travel in style. Chauffer-driven limousines are the traditional deluxe travel mode and they're still very much in fashion.

HOW TO ORDER A LIMOUSINE

The standard limousine, called format, is supplied by most services. Routinely, it comes equipped with stereo and a glass divider between driver and passengers. A few firms also supply "stretch" or Rolls Royce limousines outfitted with the works—stereo, bar and color TV.

Most firms charge from the time the limousine leaves the garage until it returns. You'll probably want to rent from someone reasonably near your home. A three hour minimum rental (plus gratuity) is required by most services, though a few have a two-hour minimum after which they charge by the quarter hour. These standard packages are based on the assumption that mileage will be within certain limits. If you exceed that mileage, charges will be by the hour and by the mile.

Our worksheet will help you make a choice. Make your reservation at least one month in advance. Most limousine services require a deposit, 1-2 weeks ahead, ranging from 50% of the total to 100%. When there is a balance, it's expected at pickup time.

Be sure you ask about cancellation policies. If cancellation is within five days of the reservation date, some firms will return your deposit. Others reserve the right to keep all or some of it.

Limousine services schedule tightly, some over a 24-hour span. Before you place your order, be sure of pickup time and place, destinations and approximate length of rental time.

OTHER TRAVEL MODES

Just about anything that moves can be used for getaway transportation—and often is! Attracted by the grace of its slower pace, many couples use a horse-drawn carriage. Antique cars and hot air balloons are favorites too. Some travel in helicopters or small, private planes. One energy-conscious pair we know peddled away on their 10-speed bikes. You're beginning a long, sentimental journey together—why not start it with flair?

PARKING

You may also find it a good idea to notify the local police department so they can decide if a traffic officer is necessary. Often, if the gathering will be held in the home or residential area, police can waive a certain restriction if given enought time in advance. At the reception, it is also nice to provide your own valet parking — eapecially if people have to walk any distance. If the reception is being held in a big city, you may want to recommend a parking garage to guests arriving from out-of-town. It may even be wise to reserve space in the garage if you anticipate a problem with availability.

NOTES

One love
that is shared by two...

DRIVER'S CHECKLIST

Name of Driver: ____________________ Vehicle: __________

Address: ____________________ Phone #: __________

PASSENGERS

1. Name: ____________________ Pick Up time: __________

   Pick Up Location: ____________________

2. Name: ____________________ Pick Up time: __________

   Pick Up Location: ____________________

3. Name: ____________________ Pick Up time: __________

   Pick Up Location: ____________________

4. Name: ____________________ Pick Up time: __________

   Pick Up Location: ____________________

5. Name: ____________________ Pick Up time: __________

   Pick Up Location: ____________________

6. Name: ____________________ Pick Up time: __________

   Pick Up Location: ____________________

Ceremony Address: ____________________ Arrival Time: __________

Directions: ____________________

____

Reception Address: ____________________ Arrival Time: __________

Directions: ____________________

____

NOTES

____

____

____

____

NOTES

The most joyous of occasions
is the union of man and woman
in the celebration of life...

Chapter 17

Reception Arrangements

The Reception

The reception is a party, a celebration of your marriage—the tone and style should reflect and complement your wedding theme. Again, planning ahead will ensure that everything goes smoothly according to your plans. The hour of the ceremony will be a guide as to the appropriate reception time to choose. Ideally, invite all your guests to both the ceremony and the reception, if possible. The reception should follow the ceremony immediately.

Once you have decided on the number of guests, the type of reception you want, and the amount of money you want to spend, you will need to choose a location. Some ideas of whom to contact are listed below:

* Fraternal organizations—try your local Moose, Elk, K of C, F.O.P., Eagles, and V.F.W. lodges. Many rent their halls to non-members. Each has its own rules and policies.
* Churches—Many have halls they will rent to members and non-members as well. Again, check on their policies.
* Country club
* Restaurants with banquet rooms—Check your local Yellow Pages.
* Ballrooms—Check your local Yellow Pages.
* Parks—Check city, county and state parks with suitable facilities.
* Home—Be sure there is enough room for everyone to move about comfortably and sufficient parking space available.
* Outdoors—You may want to rent a tent so that you have a covering over your head in case of rainy weather.

Check your local Yellow Pages for names of places to contact, or ask friends and relatives for suggestions.

Choosing the right caterer is very important. The catering expert will be able to help you choose the proper menu for the time of day your reception is being held. Generally, the caterers will supply all the dishware, flatware, glasses, cups, saucers, and table linens. They will also be able to assist you in setting up the tables and also give you ideas for decorations, etc.

The cost will largely depend on the service the caterer will provide. Some caterers will charge a flat rate or on a per-person basis. You will need to give a final estimate at least one week in advance. Be sure to get all estimates in writing.

Depending on the location you choose for your reception, you will need to make a careful decision about the liquor or other beverages you plan to serve. You will need to decide whether you want an open bar or cash bar. Then you need to decide on the types of beverages you will serve. This item is one of the major expenses of your reception.

If your reception is in a hotel or restaurant, most likely you will not be allowed to provide your own stock. Check with the banquet manager on the cost to you. If your reception is in a hall or a private home, you may have to supply your own beverages. Contact your local liquor dealer, who will be able to assist you in determining the types of liquor to serve and the quantities needed. Again, planning in advance will allow you to watch for sales on these items. Also, be sure to ask about returning unopened bottles if you do not use them.

The music at your reception will set the tone for the festivities. Once you have decided on the kind of reception you want, you will then need to determine the kind of music you want. Your choice of entertainment should be made far in advance, as the best bands are usually booked way ahead of time. Discuss with the leader the type of music you want played, as well as the kind of music you do not want. Find out how many musicians there are, what they will wear, whether or not they play continuously or take short breaks, how the rate is computed—hourly or on a set fee basis. Ask for referrals or ask to listen to them perform. Take time to go hear them at some of their next engagements. Discuss what selections you want played and when. You may also want to consider contacting a disc jockey, who can usually provide a wide variety of musical selections and may act as your master of ceremonies. Check out all the possibilities. Whatever your choice, your music will lend a happy note to your day!

The color scheme you choose for your wedding should follow through—from your attendants' dresses and flowers to the colors you choose to decorate the hall. Discuss with the manager as to what extra touches are necessary. It is often more convenient to hire someone to decorate the reception hall and dismantle it the day after as well. Your family or friends may be very willing, but it may not be convenient for them. The hall usually has some personnel available for hire.

THE HEAD TABLE AT THE RECEPTION

Naturally, the seat of honor will be yours at the main table during the reception. You will want to make the very best impression, as will the entire wedding party. Here are some helpful hints for the time when all eyes are upon you!

* Keep your voice at a moderate level, and refrain from conversation during any "little" ceremonies—when the best man is giving the newlyweds a toast, or when the clergyperson is saying a prayer before the meal, etc.
* Concentrate when you are eating—be careful so that you don't accidentally spill some food or beverage on that beautiful dress. If you're too nervous to eat, don't force yourself. But do eat something if you plan to indulge in a few ceremonial toasts.
* Keep that wedding glow about yourself—Remember you're the focus of attention for the whole crowd, the cameras, etc. Groomsmen should leave their jackets on. Bridesmaids should wait to kick off their shoes!
* Appoint a special person to wait on the head table to keep it uncluttered. A low centerpiece should be used so that it won't block anyone's view.
* If guests jointly propose a toast, try to give everyone the pleasure of acknowledging their toast by giving each other a short kiss.
* Rise to greet guests who come to offer their best wishes, and let them know how glad you are that they could come.

The wedding party should be seated as follows at the head table: the wedding party should be facing the guests so that everyone can see you. Your groom will sit to your left, your honor attendant will sit next to the groom, and the best man will go next to you. The bridesmaids and groomsmen will be seated alternately around the rest of the table. You may also wish to include the clergyperson, your parents, the groom's parents, grandparents, and godparents.

NOTES

____

____

YOUR GUEST BOOK

The guest book is a special way of preserving the names of those friends and relatives who shared your wedding day with you. Guests can also add notes of congratulations and happiness. It's a lovely keepsake to look through as the anniversaries go by.

Guest books can be purchased at any stationery or department store, or ordered through the mail. You may wish to choose a book just for guests, or a wedding memory book with a guest section. You may also want your names and the wedding date embossed on the front cover. Guest books come in many different sizes—from standard 8 1/2 x 11 to rectangles ranging from tall and thin to short and wide. White or cream-colored pages are your best choice.

The guest book should be set in a prominent place to make sure that your guests will see it and sign it. Most commonly, the guests will sign the book before or during the reception. It is suggested that you place your guest book on a nicely decorated small table near the entrance to the reception hall or at the end of the receiving line at the reception site. You may wish to designate a teenaged friend or cousin to be the guest book attendant. Your helper could direct guests to sign the book, or he/she may circulate among them to be sure everyone signs the books. It is a good idea to have a matching pen attached to the book, or on the table.

Also, if you choose a wedding memory book you will have space to collect mementos such as snapshots, newspaper clippings, etc. Make it a fun "scrapbook" to remember for a lifetime!

NOTES

RECEPTION CHECKLIST

HELD AT: ____________________ DATE: ____________________

ADDRESS: ____________________ TIME: ____________________

PHONE #: ____________________ MANAGER: ____________________

RENTAL RATE: ____________________ CANCELLATION TERMS: ___

DEPOSIT: ____________________ BALANCE DUE: ____________________

FACILITIES

WHAT CATERING SERVICES ARE PROVIDED: ______________

KITCHEN FACILITIES: ______________________________

BAR FACILITIES PROVIDED: __________________________

WHO PROVIDES AND SERVES LIQUOR: __________________

ARE TABLES AND CHAIRS PROVIDED AND QUANTITY: _____

DECORATION LIMITATIONS: ___________________________

WHEN CAN YOU GET IN TO DECORATE: _________________

ROOM CAPACITY: __________________________________

ARE YOU THE ONLY PARTY TO BE USING FACILITY THAT DAY: ______________________________

CLEAN UP REQUIREMENTS: ___________________________

PARKING FACILITIES: _______________________________

RESTROOM FACILITIES: ______________________________

NOTES

____

____

____

____

____

____

Catering Checklist

NAME: ______________________ PHONE #: ________________

ADDRESS: ___________________ REPRESENTATIVE: ________

STYLE: Buffet, Formal, Hors d'oeuvres, Cake & Punch: ________

MENUE: ____

____

____

____

____

If buffet, will bridal party be served?: ___________________________

When is final guest estimate needed?: ___________________________

Does caterer provide cake?: ___________________________

How many waiters/waitresses will be provided?: ________________

How long will they serve at the reception?: ___________________

What type of equipment does the caterer provide?: ______________

Cost

Per person: _______ Estimated Guests: _______ Cost: _______

Flat rate: ________ Estimated Guests: _______ Cost: _______

Deposit: ____________________ Balance Due: _____________

Cancellation terms: ____

Notes

____

____

____

____

____

____

ENTERTAINMENT CHECKLSIT

NAME OF GROUP: __________ PHONE #: ________________

LEADER: ____________________ TYPE OF MUSIC: __________

HOURS OF MUSIC __________ # OF BREAKS: _____________

BAND EQUIPMENT REQUIREMENTS: ______________________

COST: ____________________ DEPOSIT: ________________

CANCELLATION TERMS: _____ BALANCE: ________________

SELECTIONS

RECEIVING LINE: ____

ARRIVAL OF BRIDE & GROOM: ___________________________

DURING DINNER: ____

FIRST DANCE: ____

CAKE CUTTING: ____

THROWING OF BOUQUET: _________________________________

THROWING OF GARTER: __________________________________

LAST DANCE: ____

SPECIAL REQUESTS: ____________________________________

____

____

NOTES

____

____

____

____

____

____

____

Beverage Checklist

Bartenders

NAME:______________________ PHONE #: ________________

NAME:______________________ PHONE #: ________________

NAME:______________________ PHONE #: ________________

NAME:______________________ PHONE #: ________________

BEVERAGES PROVIDED BY: ______________________________

Open Bar Cost

ESTIMATED # OF GUESTS: _____ HOW CHARGED _______

BAR OPEN FROM:_____ TO:_____ ESTIMATED COST: _____

Cash Bar Cost

ESTIMATED # OF GUESTS: _____ HOW CHARGED _______

BAR OPEN FROM:_____ TO:_____ ESTIMATED COST: _____

Beverages Needed— Include liquor, mixers, wine, punch, etc.

KIND:______________________ QUANTITY: ______________

KIND:______________________ QUANTITY: ______________

KIND:______________________ QUANTITY: ______________

KIND:______________________ QUANTITY: ______________

KIND:______________________ QUANTITY: ______________

KIND:______________________ QUANTITY: ______________

KIND:______________________ QUANTITY: ______________

EQUIPMENT NEEDED:____________________________________

____

____

____

____

Reception Decoration Checklist

Head Table

TYPE:____________________ SOURCE:____________________

Cake Table

TYPE:____________________ SOURCE:____________________

Buffet Table

TYPE:____________________ SOURCE:____________________

Guest Table

TYPE:____________________ SOURCE:____________________

Other

TYPE:____________________ SOURCE:____________________

Notes

Rental Checklist

RENTAL AGENCY ____________ PHONE#: ____________

ADDRESS: ____________ REPRESENTATIVE ____________

DELIVERY DATE: ____________ PICK UP DATE: ____________

Items Rented

ITEM: ____________ COST: ____________

ITEM: ____________ COST: ____________

ITEM: ____________ COST: ____________

ITEM: ____________ COST: ____________

ITEM: ____________ COST: ____________

ITEM: ____________ COST: ____________

DEPOSIT: ____________ BALANCE DUE: ____________

Notes

____

____

____

____

____

____

____

____

____

____

____

____

____

____

NOTES

This day
I will marry
my best friend,
The one I
laugh with,
live for, love...

Chapter 18

Wedding Cake

THE WEDDING CAKE

The wedding cake is as important as the bridal veil, gown, rings, etc. It may be as artistic—and sometimes as fantastic—as a designer's dream. It is usually decorated with intricate designs. The cake is sometimes placed as a centerpiece on the bridal table if there is one; if not, the cake sits on its own table with perhaps a color coordinated table cloth so that it may be admired by everyone; or it may also form the centerpiece for a buffet table.

Wedding cakes may be square, oblong, or heart-shaped, but are usually a series of round tiers, sometimes separated by columns. The icing is usually white, but the cake can be frosted with a pastel icing to match the color scheme of your wedding. Usually an ornament, or fresh flowers, finishes off the top layer; or what is known as a "cake top." The cake itself is made of a white pound cake or a yellow sponge cake—or you may want to be creative and have each layer be a different flavor. But try to stick to the basics.

The less familiar groom's cake is a dark, rich fruitcake, frequently iced to match and used as the top layer of the bride's cake. Traditionally, this cake is saved for the first anniversary of the couple. Because tradition has it that a piece of the bride's cake under a single woman's pillow will lead her to dream of her future husband, it's customary to cut the cake and serve it at the reception, with extra slices provided for guests to take home. Napkins or tiny boxes are supplied to those who wish to take pieces of cake home with them. If you won't be having a groom's cake, freeze the top layer of the bride's cake to share on your first anniversary.

In some traditions, the dark fruitcake is the main wedding cake (English). The pieces are all pre-cut with perhaps an almond on top, wrapped in cellophane and topped with a bow for guests to take home if they choose. An artificial cake is then sometimes used for the photographs.

ORDERING THE CAKE

If you need ideas of what kind of cake you would like, why not ask some of your friends who were recently married, or look through photo albums at your local bakeries or caterers. Before you order, it is wise to taste a sample of their baking. Keep in mind that, generally speaking, not much cake is eaten at weddings. You don't want to have much left over and wasted. It is suggested that you order a cake that "looks" big, but really isn't.

It's also a good idea to make a check list of points to go over:

* Discuss number of guests.
* Shape and size of cake
* Batter (flavor)
* Filling
* Icing (colors)
* Designs
* Ornaments (cake top)
* Total price
* Deposit
* Time and date of delivery (if they deliver)

If you're thinking of making your own cake, keep in mind that the time right before your big day is the most hectic. Before you go ahead, check the cost of ingredients against the price of a professionally prepared cake. Then experiment with your recipe way ahead of time, and make the real thing at least two days before you decorate it; it's easier to ice when it's not too fresh.

NOTES

____

____

____

____

____

____

____

____

____

____

____

____

Cutting the Cake

The wedding cake should be cut just before dessert at a luncheon or dinner reception, just after the guests have been received at a tea or cocktail reception. Your groom places his right hand over yours and together you cut into the bottom layer with a ribbon-tied silver knife. The bride and groom traditionally share the first slice as a symbol of their willingness to share each other's household from then on.

It is a loving gesture for the bride to give her new in-laws their pieces after that, then the groom to service his. The rest of the cake is then cut by a friend, designated in advance, or by a member of the caterer's staff, and served to the guests.

Use a thin, sharp or serrated knife. Insert knife into cake, keeping point down and handle up. Slice, pulling knife toward you. If frosting sticks, dip knife in hot water or wipe with damp paper towel after cutting each slice.

Round Tiered Cake

A. Cut vertically through bottom layer at edge of second layer as indicated by dotted line 1; then cut into wedges as indicated by dotted line 2.

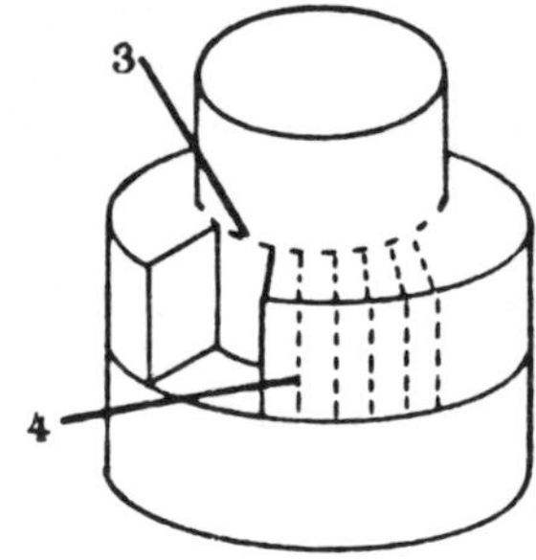

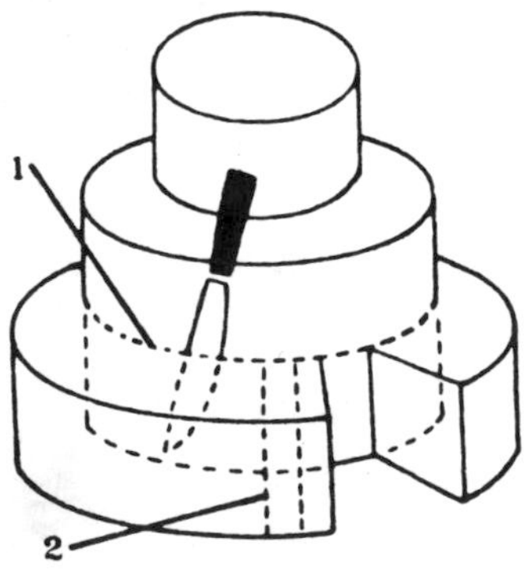

B. Follow same procedure with middle layer by cutting vertically through second layer at edge of top layer as indicated by dotted line 3; then cut into wedges as indicated by dotted line 4.

C. Return to bottom layer and cut along dotted line 5; cut into wedges as indicated by dotted line 6.

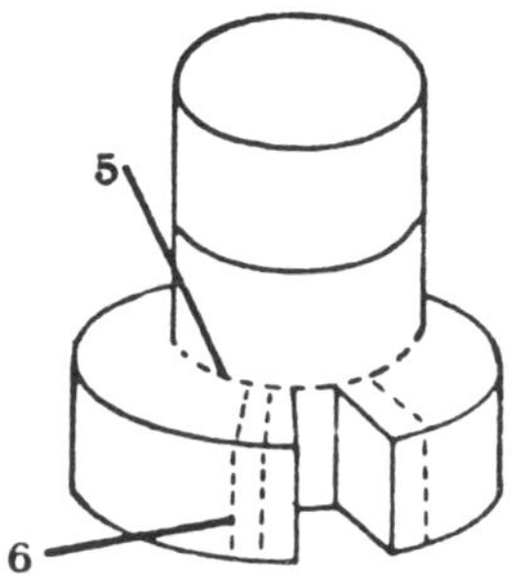

D. Separate remaining layers (traditionally, the top layer is frozen for the couple's first anniversary); cut into desired sizes.

E. Round layers can be cut into wedges, diamonds or slices.

SQUARE TIERED CAKE

The cutting procedure for square tiered cake is essentially the same as for a round tiered cake. Cut bottom layer all around; then cut middle layer. Return to bottom layer and continue as directed (above).

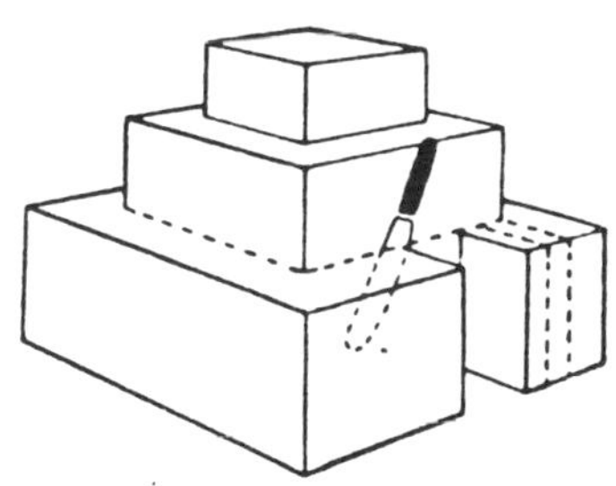

NOTES

NOTES

The first day of
our life together...

Chapter 19

Honeymoon

THE HONEYMOON

You should plan your honeymoon together—discuss how much money you can afford to spend, the length of time you can take for your honeymoon, and where you would like to go. It is best to plan the honeymoon well in advance, so that you both can start to save toward the kind of honeymoon you really want. Both the availability of funds and the location chosen for your honeymoon will help determine the length of your trip. Also, be sure you can get away from your place of employment. Do you have vacation time coming or will you have to take time off without pay? If your vacation isn't due at the time you are getting married, you may want to postpone your honeymoon for awhile.

In planning your honeymoon, discuss what both of you like to do. Write for brochures from resorts, hotels, etc. Contact a good travel agent who can provide you with information on special package deals, airline fares, hotel reservations, etc. A travel agent can also help you get the most for your time and money.

HELPFUL TIPS

Given below is a helpful guide in planning your honeymoon:

* How long do you want to be away on your honeymoon?
* Do you want to be economical or can you afford to splurge?
* How much do you want to spend?
* How far do you want to travel?
* Do you want to fly, drive, or take a cruise?
* Do you want to spend the major part of your honeymoon in a sophisticated city, a small town, a big resort, or a small hideaway?
* Do you want a honeymoon package, a group tour, or an independent itinerary tailor-made just for the two of you?
* Do you want to stay in an isolated, self-contained resort, or a hotel that's right in the middle of the action?
* Do you want to do some sightseeing, learn a new sport, shop for bargains, study something, or just simply relax?
* Do you want to leave the continental U.S.?

Once you have decided on where you want to go, you will need to know what to take with you:

* Coordinate your honeymoon attire with your fiance so you have the appropriate clothing, whether you are going hiking or dining, and so that you look like you really belong together.
* Take with you any reservation confirmations or deposit slips.
* Make sure you have necessary tickets.
* Label luggage with names, address and phone number, both inside and outside.
* Try to use traveler's checks or credit cards instead of carrying large sums of cash.
* Take proper identification with you—driver's license, birth certificate, etc.
* If travelling abroad, be sure you have your passport or visa in order.
* Check on insurance—whether it covers your belongings while on a trip. If not, buy additional insurance.

After all the excitement of planning the wedding, and the wedding day itself, you will need some time to just relax and enjoy each other! You might want to give consideration, therefore, to a more quiet time so that you aren't exhausted from running the whole time.

NOTES

Honeymoon Checklist
Wedding Night

HOTEL:__________ LOCATION: __________

ARRIVAL TIME: __________ DEPARTURE TIME:__________

Travel Agency

NAME:__________ PHONE #: __________

ADDRESS: __________ REPRESENTATIVE:__________

Honeymoon Location

NAME OF HOTEL: __________ PHONE #: __________

ADDRESS: __________

ARRIVAL DATE & TIME: __________

DEPARTURE DATE & TIME: __________

Transportation

MODE:__________ PICK UP TICKETS: __________

DEPARTURE DATE & TIME: __________

ARRIVAL DATE & TIME: __________

CAR RENTAL AGENCY: __________ ADDRESS: __________

Costs

HOTEL __________

TRANSPORTAITON __________
MISCELLANEOUS __________
(Food, entertainment, souvenirs, etc.)

TOTAL: __________

Love is as certain
As the tide whispering on the shore

NOTES

NOTES

Love fills the moment
and the moment begins eternity.
Love fills a lifetime
and a lifetime begins this hour

Chapter 20

Summary Checklist

The Rings

___ Have you picked up your wedding rings?
___ Do the rings fit properly?
___ Is the engraving correct?
___ Have you insured your rings?

Newspaper Announcements

___ Have you completed the wedding announcement information form completely?
___ Have you sent the form and glossy photo to your newspaper?
___ Have you confirmed with the newspaper that it has been received?
___ Will it appear at the designated time?

The Ceremony

___ Have all details of the ceremony been finalized with the officiating clergyperson?
___ Have all musical selections been made?
___ Have all final details been made with the organist, musicians, and soloist?
___ Have decorations for the ceremony been finalized?
___ Does the florist know which arrangements are to be delivered to the ceremony site?
___ Does the rental agency know what items are to be delivered to the ceremony site?
___ Does the rental agency know the delivery date, time and place?
___ Do the wedding party and musicians (and any other special assistants) know the date, time, and place of the rehearsal and rehearsal dinner?
___ Have all arrangements been made for the rehearsal dinner?
___ Does the best man know that he will be delivering the fee to the officiating clergyperson?
___ Do all the attendants and ushers know their duties?

Love is beautiful simply
by being what it is.

THE RECEPTION

___ Have you finalized all the details with the person in charge at the reception site?
___ Have you checked on seating and table arrangements at the reception site?
___ Have you finalized all details with the baker? Does he/she know the delivery date, time and place?
___ Have you made arrangements for someone to cut the cake?
___ Do you have a cake knife?
___ Have all details been finalized with the caterer? Have you given the caterer a final estimate of number of guests?
___ Have you checked on beverage supplies?
___ Will there be enough waiters/waitresses and bartenders to serve your guests?
___ Have you finalized details with the rental agency? Do they know delivery date, time and place?
___ Did you finalize details with the band?
___ Have you decided whether or not you will be throwing the bouquet or garter?
___ Have you finalized arrangements with the florist as far as decoration for the reception site? Do they know delivery date, time and place?
___ Do you have someone to be in charge of the guest book?

WEDDING PARTY ATTIRE

___ Is your wedding attire in order—dress, headpiece, and accessories?
___ Are your bridesmaids' dresses ready?
___ Does everything fit properly? Have they been picked up or delivered?
___ Is the mens' formal wear ready?
___ Do the parents' have their attire?
___ Have you purchased gifts for attendants?
___ Have you made an appointment at the beauty salon?

How beautiful is the day
that is touched by
Love

The Photographer

___ Have you finalized all details with the photographer? Does he/she know the date, time and location of your home, ceremony and reception?
___ Have you provided the photographer with a list of special pictures you want taken during the ceremony and reception?

The Florist

___ Have you made a final check with your florist? Are all your choices of flowers acceptable?
___ Does your florist know which flowers are to be delivered where and when?

Transportation

___ Have you finalized all arrangements for transportation? Do you have enough vehicles?
___ Do the drivers know their schedules and whom they are to pick up?

The Printer

___ Have you ordered invitations, thank you cards, napkins, etc.?
___ Did you order wedding programs?
___ Do you have a guest book?
___ Have you proofread all printed materials?

Legal Matters

___ Do you have your marriage license?
___ Have arrangements been made to change your name on all important documents?

The Honeymoon

___ Have all reservations been confirmed for both the wedding night and the wedding trip—transportation and hotels?
___ Do you have all your tickets?
___ Have you left a schedule of your plans with your parents or friends?
___ Did you pick up travelers' checks?
___ If travelling abroad, did you exchange for foreign currency?
___ Did you have your car checked out for the trip?
___ Did you arrange for someone to check your home while you are gone?

This day
Our hearts are
Joined as One

Chapter 21

Questions Most Commonly Asked

QUESTIONS MOST COMMONLY ASKED

WHAT DO WE DO IF OUR PARENTS ARE DIVORCED?

Although this can be an awkward moment for everyone, the most important point to remember is in considering everybody's feelings. The approach depends upon your relationship with the entire family—parents and stepparents. Communication is the solution. Discuss your feelings with them and listen to their objections. Each situation is unique. Try to remain sensitive and then proceed with arrangements that allow everyone to participate with grace. Keep in mind that you cannot change the divorce, and the success of **your** wedding is your ultimate goal.

Consider who is sponsoring the wedding. If they are absolutely unwilling to be civil, you must simply keep them apart. Most often, they will overlook their feelings for the sake of your feelings and your wedding day.

The reception is more relaxed and less structured. Most seating arrangements can be dealt with at this level as everyone is more at ease. The ceremony is much more delicate and therefore guidelines for seating will reduce the amount of anxiety or tension.

If your parents are divorced, but not remarried, if they are congenial, they might sit together in the left front row at Christian weddings; women sit on the left and men on the right at Jewish ceremonies. Otherwise your mother sits in the left front pew and your father sits in the third row on the left side. (This is also an individual decision.)

When each parent has remarried, your mother sits in the customary place with her husband, and your father sits with his wife in the third left-hand row.

If you happen to be living with your father and stepmother who are sponsoring the wedding, they sit in the front row. Then your mother and stepfather, as honored guests, sit in the third left-hand row.

If your brother or uncle is taking the place of your absent father, he sits with your mother. The same would apply to anyone substituting for your mother.

Seat your groom's divorced parents in identical position, but in the right-hand rows.

WHAT DO WE DO IF THIS IS A SECOND MARRIAGE?

A second wedding should not appear to be duplicating or competing with the first. When both the bride and groom remarry, the ceremony is traditionally small and informal with the bride and her party dressed in elegant, but not formal "bridal" attire. This is not always followed. Many couples who are remarrying have a much more monumental wedding. They may even include their children in the actual ceremony, which is actually quite healthy when reuniting the "family" unit. Also, it helps to include them rather than give them the feeling of exclusion and insecurity.

If one of you is marrying for the first time, a traditional wedding is probably the answer. However, compromise is often the key and communication the means to achieve your decision. Usually, in a remarriage, the couples are paying for the wedding themselves so financial guidelines will dictate the type of wedding you will have.

Be sure to consult with your church and clergyperson regarding a second marriage. You must be sure to realize that some churches/denominations are reluctant to marry divorced persons. This may also direct you in the type of wedding you will have.

WHAT ROLES DO THE STEPCHILDREN PLAY?

It is recommended that you ask your children their preference and opinion regarding the wedding. The children should be made to feel like an important member of the new family. Keep them informed of your plans from the very beginning.

These decisions depend upon the child's age. If they are too young or the wedding will be small, give each child a variety of responsibilities to fulfill. Some ideas are: filling the champagne glasses, cutting the cake and serving, assisting the guests in signing the guest book, checking coats, and also to participate in the church service itself.

HOW DO I CHOOSE MY NAME?

Traditionally, a bride always took her husband's name. It is actually a custom rather than a law. Today, many women have a greater sense of self-identity and/or possibly have built a professional reputation prior to their wedding, and thus, elect to retain their own last name. You do retain the same legal rights regardless of your choice. In fact, you have the legal right to use any name as long as you can show it wasn't changed for any illegal purposes. Make your choice early. It is much easier to change it at the time of marriage than it is to change it later on.

HERE ARE SOME POINTS TO REMEMBER:

1) Maintain your own credit record. Although equal credit laws are on the books, you must do your part. If you keep **your** name on any credit cards, be sure they stay in **your** name if it's different.
2) Keep in mind that someday you may want to open your own business or co-sign a mortgage loan. Maintain your own bank and charge accounts. If you open joint accounts, insist that creditors keep separate credit files in each name.

RETAINING SINGLE NAME

1) Be sure to travel with a copy of your marriage certificate at all times. This can clarify any question to the validity of your surname.
2) The easiest manner to follow is to use your married name socially, but your birth name professionally. Don't apologize to those who question you, but be gracious. You do have the right to decide how you shall be called.

USING BOTH NAMES

1) It is a compromise of sorts when you use both names because you are retaining your single name and adding your husband's name (i.e. Mary Smith Doe).
2) A more complex name change is the hyphenated name (i.e. Mary Smith-Doe). In fact, some grooms are doing it too (i.e. John Doe-Smith or John Smith-Doe).
   Today's business people are apt to assume a bride is retaining her single name. If you're making a change, it is a nice idea to send a card to associates to inform them of your decision.

Ms. Mary Smith
announces she has adopted the surname of
Doe

Another idea is to enclose a card with your wedding invitation or mail one separately.

Mary Smith and John Doe
wish to announce that both
will be retaining their present names
for all legal and social purposes
after their marriage
June 15, 1988

Eventually, of course, people will learn your preference through word of mouth. This could be enhanced by your wedding announcement in the newspaper.

Following is a simple checklist for areas requiring a name change. They may require a copy of your marriage license with notification. You may want to check by phone before writing.

Driver's license
Car registration
Social Security
Voter's registration
Passport
Bank accounts
Credit cards
Insurance policies
School and/or employer's records
Post offices
Employment records
Pension plans
Stocks
Bonds
Property titles
Leases
Wills
Beneficiaries

IF I AM AN OLDER BRIDE, CAN I STILL FOLLOW TRADITION?

Simply stated, yes. Your wedding is as special as any other. Plan it in your very own style. Your biggest advantage is that you and he have been on your own for many years and you'll probably be paying your own wedding expenses; therefore, you won't have any obligation to consult with or compromise with others. You may decide to forgo some of the less dignified social practices, but your "bridal" attire is strictly up to you.

WHAT IS THE CUSTOMARY PROCESS FOR REAFFIRMING YOUR VOWS?

If you married in haste and later regret that you missed all the ceremony and celebration, all you have to do is retrace your steps and start over again. Renew those vows or have a special blessing in a very nice church setting with all the necessary trimmings...including a big reception. This idea is becoming a popular idea for a wedding anniversary, perhaps a silver or golden. Many times the couple's children and grandchildren participate in the ceremony. An indication of this can be a part of the anniversary invitation as well.

HOW DO WE CHOOSE OUR HOME...YOUR PLACE, MY PLACE?

The ideal solution is our place. This usually means someplace neutral. If this is not possible, give thought to some simple redecorating or remodeling that could be done to one place or the other. If there are children involved, that must be given first consideration (i.e. schools, playmates, security, etc.). And of course, financial abilities must also be considered.

Trying to merge two households requires much patience any way you look at it. After years of making your own decisions, two independent people pledge to share their life together. It takes more than love to make a successful merger. It requires a great deal of tolerance, negotiation, and mutual respect. Communication is always important, and with enough compromise you will reach a decision that allows you both to be comfortable.

This may also be the best time to draw up an inventory, listing every piece. Compare items, combine, and dispose of what is not needed. This is perfect for insurance purposes as well as personal records. Those items which you don't need can be sold, given to family or given to a charitable organization. And, anything that you cannot decide what to do with...well, just simply toss a coin.

DO WE NEED A MARRIAGE CONTRACT?

A marriage contract is something to consider if you need to define or express differently any right in your marriage that is customarily taken for granted. Many states are now community property states. Consult a lawyer beforehand. As unromantic as this may sound, a marriage contract can serve as a good format to begin on, thereby paving the way to a healthier, happier future. You will find that the Jewish weddings have implied this for centuries.

NOTES

NOTES

Two lives, two hearts
joined together in friendship
united forever in
Love

Chapter 22

Protecting Your Valuables

Protecting Your Wedding Gifts and Other Valuables

A few simple precautions will help you protect your belongings for now and for the future. Gifts you receive from friends and family will certainly have some sentimental worth, as well as cash value—so protect those valuables before, during, and after the wedding!

It is suggested that you take out insurance to cover anticipated gifts. A "wedding present floater" is a special policy covering anything that won't stay in one place. The homeowners' insurance held by your parents, for instance, probably won't protect any gifts gathered in their house that you will move to your apartment. The "floater" is good for a temporary period—usually about 90 days after the wedding. It gives "blanket coverage," meaning that you don't have to list each item you're insuring, since you really don't know what gifts will be coming in. You're protected against theft, fire, breakage, etc. There's seldom a deductible which would have you picking up part of any loss. You get back the total value.

If you already own or rent the home that you will live in, you will need regular coverage. A smarter investment, then, would be a homeowners' or renters' policy to cover all of your possessions. If you already have this type of insurance, you should "up" your coverage to include any new items you will be receiving or purchasing. For example, if your current policy is good for $7,000, you may want to "up" it an additional $2,000 to cover the gifts that you will be receiving for your wedding. Also, be sure to check with your insurance agent to see what exactly is covered.

Recording and keeping track of all your possessions and gifts may seem tedious, but it is wise to take the time to do this. Your "Wedding Gift Register" is one of your most valuable assets. It provides you with the name and address of the gift giver, the date of acknowledgement, the item given, and the place of purchase. The "register" is your best resource for future fill-ins or replacement and evaluation for insurance purposes. When a claim is filed on a theft loss, the insurance company requires documentation of ownership. If you do not have a household inventory, receipts showing purchase are acceptable proof. However, newlyweds do not have receipts for their wedding gifts, but if you keep good documentation in your "register" you may use this for documentation of ownership.

You must also have record of all personal possessions owned by both of you before your marriage, and items purchased by you after you were married.

An inventory of everything you own, including gifts received at showers, etc., should be taken before the wedding so that you know how much coverage you will need. All items should be recorded, indicating their cash value and age if it is a family heirloom or antique. You may wish to consult a professional appraiser for some items. Be certain your engagement ring and wedding rings have an up-to-date appraisal. The value of gold, silver, and jewels changes constantly.

When taking your inventory be sure to include clothing, sports or hobby equipment, furniture, appliances, etc. If you can find receipts for any of your items, collect them and put them in an envelope to keep on file. Also, it is a good practice to take photos of all your possessions. You should put identifying numbers on all items that can be engraved. Contact your local police department for more information on identification numbers. This practice deters thieves.

After your inventory has been taken and a list is made, you should make a copy for your records, and store the original in a safe-deposit box. Also, update your records from time to time.

If all this seems unnecessary and tedious, total up the cash value of all the items on your inventory and see what an investment it represents. Does the amount surprise you? Once you realize the value of these belongings, you will probably want to take steps to assure the safety of your precious possessions! With a little thoughtful planning, the things you love can be with you for a lifetime.

...And this
Our Life,
Our
Beginning

Shakespeare

REMEMBERING THE ANNIVERSARIES

First	Paper
Second	Cotton
Third	Leather
Fourth	Books
Fifth	Wood
Sixth	Iron
Seventh	Copper
Eighth	Electric
Ninth	Pottery
Tenth	Tin
Eleventh	Steel
Twelfth	Linen
Thirteenth	Lace
Fourteenth	Ivory
Fifteenth	Crystal
Twentieth	China
Twenty-fifth	Silver
Thirtieth	Pearl
Thirty-fifth	Coral
Fortieth	Ruby
Forty-fifth	Sapphire
Fiftieth	Gold
Fifty-fifth	Emerald
Sixtieth	Diamond

PLEASE SEND ME YOUR COMMENTS. MAKE SUGGESTIONS OR OFFER CRITISISM. WE WOULD LOVE TO HEAR FROM YOU IN OUR EFFORTS TO CONTINUALLY IMPROVE BRIDAL GUIDE, A COMPLETE GUIDE ON HOW TO PLAN A WEDDING. THANK-YOU.

FOR A FRIEND

NAME: ____

ADDRESS: ____

____

____

WEDDING DATE ______________ TELEPHONE ___________

COMMENTS ____

____

____

____

____

____

____

For additional copies send $12.95 plus $2.50 shipping and handling to:

BRIDAL GUIDE, LTD.
c/o Pamela Thomas—author
P.O. BOX 2091
La Crosse, WI 54602-2091
(608) 788-5772

Master Card/Visa #: _________________________________

Exp. date: ____

Signature ____